Along Life's Road

Book 3

Poetry, Songs and Stories

**Written By Albert E. Vicent
Compiled By Haruka Vicent
And Michael Vicent
Cover Photo By Albert C. Vicent**

Order this book online at www.trafford.com
or email orders@trafford.com

Most Trafford titles are also available at major online book retailers.

Print information available on the last page.

ISBN: 978-1-4907-7103-8 (sc)
ISBN: 978-1-4907-7102-1 (e)

Trafford rev. 03/11/2016

 www.trafford.com

North America & international
toll-free: 1 888 232 4444 (USA & Canada)
fax: 812 355 4082

Road

A Road
How it travels
From here
And there too.
As if planned
To travel
Far-near
Thru.
Then here-there
For you, others
And me too.
Along the road a road-that road
That road of life.

Poems

Lovely Eternal

I see the sun it lights the day
I see the twilight
It lights the evening
With soft light
Then the evening
Comes and welcomes night
And the moon the stars
With their glowing
Soft near far away
Mysterious twinkling light
I see them I watch them
They fascinate me
I'm sure they have fascinated others
Many others too thru the creators
Wondrous years
Given freely to use
In individual chosen ways
And then the night
The night moon stars
With their far ways
Near mysterious and
Twinkling light
Welcome the dawn and the sun
That lights each day
In a silent lovely eternal way
I see them I feel them
And blessed I am
With them
Everyday the creator gives me
Blessed beautiful each day
And each with love in
Just lovely, lovely
ways.

Long Time Ago

Twas a long long time ago
It seems now so
I remember when the old
Steam trains used to go
With their whistles a blowin
Bells a ringin
Cars clackity, clackity
Clackin by
Seems like they were
Big snortin whistling
Monsters goin by
When I was a child
I can remember them
Got quite fond of em too
In the little small town
of Peacock in Michigan
Where they would come crossin the old
Gravel road
Where the old cars
The old wooden spoked
Model T Ford's, Essex, a few
Model A's and others would go,
Putt putt kickin up
A little dust passin by
Seemed like they the cars
Was a flyin course now
I know now they wasn't
A goin that fast
And the trains
They were just makin old
Steam train noise a huffin a puffin
A blowin a makin steam
Train noises
Wish I could hear it now
Just a passin one more time
A passin a passin
Just a passin with the time
Thru those old steam trains
And the old cars too...Like,
A long, long time ago
A passin, a passin, just,
A, passin thru.

Changed

To open the window
Or open the door
Let in the sunlight
Day light or night
Nothing has changed
But all is not as before
Yet...
Everything has changed
Take a deep breath let the outside in
The inside out
To pray to the creator
Is much the same
Nothing changes tho
All does too in its way
The inside is out the outside is in
When to pray if in the heart
One is true alone in its way
Comes thru to your new openly
As to open a window or door
You just let in new light lovely light
To you.

Memorial Day

Today's the day Memorial day
We've set aside
To honor those who were
In past right by our side
But now have left to go beyond
The creator called them,
When called all must respond
Today's a holiday
Flowers flags parades visitation
Picnics but most of all
By and thru
Remembering visiting
Decorating cleaning
Places in cemeteries
To honor those who were
In past right by our side
Now left for beyond the other side
When the creator
Called we remember them today
On Memorial Day

Each Day

So lovely the way
Dawn beckons
Morning to come aboard
Morning noon
Noon twilight
Twilight evening
Evening night
Night the dawn
So lovely the way
Dawn beckons
Beckons life's way
Each day

A Lizard

I seen a little lizard
And then it ran away
I seen a little lizard today.

Calleth

Get up get up get up
Today calleth
Get up get up get up
Get up
Today calleth
Get up and see
Today
Today's way
Today calleth

Walking

Turn the page
Keep walking on
Thru the days and
Thru the nights
Thru the morning
Noon's twilight
thru books read
Then re read too
Memorized
In forehead back
Right thru
One must
Turn the page
Keep walking
On always, always, keep walking-
walking on.

Known

For the many years
Our families have known
Each other
For the many trials
And happiness together
We've been thru
We continually thank
The creator of the universe
For all and the love shared
Daily too
And now that the sun is setting
In the creators special way
We ask of the creator
For we all to continue
Thru family love and
Always the creators love daily
Also with thanks for
Our many years together
Creations way and,
The...Creators way.

Elephant

Oh look up at the sky
At the clouds in the sky
You can see an elephant
Riding by with a trunk
In the front and a tail
In the back riding by
On a tricycle
In the clouds
Way
Up in the sky.

Vessels

We are earthen vessels
Made from dust of earth
Containing a glory
Of wonderful story
As a seed a
Glory an achievement
Of the creator with love
For all to behold
a story told
Large very large
We are earthen vessels
Made from earth
Creations story
Filled with the creators glory.

Leaves

The leaves are here today
I like the leaves
The leaves on trees
The leaves came quiet
And to my tree leaves come
Some I did not see but
I like the leaves
The leaves are here today
The leaves are here today.

Strange

People, people strange they are
If they walk – they want a car
If get a car- they want to walk
And if live in the country- the city is nice
If travel by plane- the trains to slow
If travel by train – the planes too fast
People, people tho strange they be
Being in that way-
They are … the people, people, people-
People, that they are.

Again

Try to remember again
So that nothing may be lost
The beauty of a sunset
The beauty of a frost
The beauty of a moment
Spent with a love
A love of lovely known only
To those truly
Of love
Try to remember
To remember again
For memory as a season
As a beautiful lovely reason
Changes fleets returns again
With more or less or more
Try to remember again
So that nothing may be lost.

Bunch

There goes a bunch of birds
They are flying altogether
They are flying this way that way
Everyway
Or other
Oh there they go
Flying far way
Where every one goes
When they are just
Going this way or that way
Everyway
Or other.

Till

Up the hill when you're young
Down the hill when you're old
Over the hill when you're really really old
And then
On the level is where you're traveling then
If you do
If you do
Till
You're thru
Ain't travelin grand
Up the hills
Down the hills
Over the hills
On the level too
All the way thru.

The Ocean

Go…
Down to the ocean
Where the ocean birds stay
Where the shores are long
Where tides come go away
Where ships can be seen
Near far away
Where the water meets the sky
And the sky
Tho you travel is always…
Far away
There the ocean speaks in tones
Tones it knows
Knows alone
Soft to a baby's ear sometimes
Roars as lions do at times go,
Down to the ocean
See…
Where the water of the ocean
And the sky meet
Then flow on, on, on
Rippling, thundering, crashing, and…
With mystery on to shores of
The far far…. Far away.

Cookies

Cookies, cookies,cookies
Cookies will thrill you
Cookies will kill you
Cookies make the whole world nice
While cookies just thrill you
On the way to paradise
Cookies, cookies, cookies.

Traveled

As one travels
Far and wide to see the world
Thru travel
Thru its many ways
A holy book a bible too
Is there for many
Who choose to seek its advice
To guide the way
That everyday
Will help much
And guide with love
Show the way guide the way
As stars above if used
Will guide
I've used and use it daily too
This book and found it
To be true
In my travels of the
World I've seen
And traveled thru.

Obvious

The house may not be beautiful
The path may not be clean
The book its cover
Torn
But
The house its garden is beautiful
The path leads on
To arrive beautiful
The book is filled
With knowledge yet to behold
If we but see beyond
the exterior obvious, and-
To inner love. Where
There's beauty. There's beautiful.

Weapons

The police are firing weapons
At a firing range nearby
Pop, pop, pop the weapons go
and the lead at the targets
Just goes, it-
Flies, flies, flies.

The Circle

The circle gets smaller
Of folks one knows
Or at least it somehow
Seems that way
As one gets older then older
Day by day and the hours
Of 24 each day
Are the same they come that way
Interesting too tho they do
But the circle one sees
Gets smaller more small
The creator must have designed it that way
As the days flow gently their way
The cycle continues
The circle does too
Smaller, smaller its way each
24 hours per day
As it flows gently silently
Thru.

For Fun

Don't use guns
For fun
Guns protect you
That
They'll do
Guns will harm
Your neighbors too
Don't use guns for fun
Cause…
You or somebody else
Might kill you
Or…
Your neighbors
Too. With guns.

Old Clock

On the wall
On the wall
Old clock on the wall
You tell us you're with us
When you stop you're away
Evenings seasons
Nights and days
War time and peace time
Travelin too
In everything you're there
Till its thru
On the wall on the wall
Old clock on the wall
Just tickin and tickin
And tickin
Tickin the hours away.

The Clouds

There come the clouds
Covering the sky
The blue of sky
The sunshine too
Just it seems
To make a cloudy day
For no apparent reason
The day was nice
For this season
Its way
I thought it was nice
The clouds didn't
They are changing it
To their way
There come the clouds
To change
The day their way.

Sweet

Cookies are sweet
Cookies are sweet
Cookies are good to eat
If you like something
Sweet to eat…
Cookies are good to eat.

Viewing

The view across a valley
Under blue of sky
With scattered clouds
Drifting over its hills
Offers a wondrous
Beautiful viewing
Of natures paintings of
Upon the hills
Just viewing across the valley
The clouds... blue sky
And o'er the hills.

Try it

To one
It means a lot to
Drive to a spot
Where its quiet out in the country
And watch the clouds
And blue of sky
The horizon where it
Meets mountain tops
Green hills and trees grow...
Till it seems they kind of
Never stop
Houses too scattered
Here and there in a valley
On hillsides too
This means a lot of me
To be able to do
And see
Try it sometime
You might like it too
I do of course
I'm almost eighty three.

In the Sky

I hear an airplane overhead
Just roaring roaring
In the sky going by
Another large ,large passenger
Plane I see
Gliding slow just
Getting low in the sky
I see too in the heavens so
Cloudy blue
Airplanes passing landing too
Birds they seem the same
To do
Airplanes birds they, I think
Help fill the sky
For I most everyday
Hear them roaring see them
Silent in the sky just-
Going, going by, going by.

Almost

Pears and apples
Are really nice fruit
Smell nice
Have almost the same kind
Of seeds
But are different indeed
The fruit.

Crawling

Little bugs on the floor
Crawling round and round
Then more
Do you ever hear the sounds
Of wind and rain
See the sun rise in the sky
See evening night time
Passing by
Or do you just hear the tramp ,tramp, tramping
Of feet as they pass by
Little bugs on the floor, you may fear-
Crawling round and round
Then more
What sounds do you hear
There on the floor?
Or are the shadows, bugs, shadows-
Just something
That you fear more, more then more.

The Winds

The afternoon winds
Make the leaves on the trees
Rustle and the limbs
Dance a little too
I think the trees
Like the winds as the winds
Passes thru.

Light

So bright the lights
In dark of night
They light the dark
With bright of light
And the dark is bright then
The night is bright with light

So Peaceful

Way over, over there
At the horizon
Where the mountain top
Meets the sky
Where the mountain appears
Blue to the eye
It seems so peaceful and silent
To the eye
I wonder if I were there
Would over here
Seems the same from
Over there as over there
Seems from over here
I've never been over there
Have you, ever been
Over there/
Way over there
At the horizon
Where the mountain top
Meets the sky ?

Camping

Camping is something
Some people like some people don't
Camping is something
If you try and you like it
Then you do
Camping is something
If you try it and you don't like it
Then you won't
Camping is something
Some people like, some people don't
I like camping
How about you?
Do you like camping too?
Or don't you?

Peaceful

From where I can see
There's a little town I can see
In the valley below
That looks peaceful to me
There's green of grass
Streets houses too
Soft lights by night
Quiets there too
Of course I'm quite sure
All is not always quiet there,
Nice as can be
But…
From where and what
I can see
There's a little town
In the valley below
That looks peaceful to me.

Soaring

I just seen two birds fighting in the sky
They were two large graceful flying birds
The type of birds I see
Usually soaring gliding
Peaceful, hunting from the sky
Today I seen much unrest between
Those two birds
I seen in the sky today
Only one bird
Of the two flew away
Birds I assume
Have their form of justice too
Effective silent in the sky
I just seen two birds
Fighting in the sky.

Large Spider

There's a large spider I see
Painted on a tree stays
Always in the same place
Quiet as can be
It never moves up
It never moves down
It never moves at all
Or even crawls around
There a large spider I see
Painted on a tree
Always in the same place
Quiet as can be.

Evening Breeze

The evening breeze
Brings cool of air
Twilight long shadows
Evening night, with dark
Is here and dark will stay
Till dawn brings day
The evening breeze brings cool of air
Long shadows twilight near

Evening

Twilight time long shadows near
Evenings, on its way
Night time too
Dark soon will be here
Stars and moon will fill the sky
Night will be till dawn is nigh
The moon will rule the sky
Dawn will bring the light of day
And sun will rule the day
But now is
Twilight time, long shadows near
Evenings on its way.

Birds

I watch the birds
Many settling in the trees
Nearby to stay
For the night
Till day comes nigh
The trees don't mind
For the tress have room
And will share with the birds
Till the night passes by
And day comes nigh
I watch the birds
Many settling in the tress
Its interesting to me.

Thought Unseen

Standing almost still
In the air some birds
Can stay and move their wings
Ever so slight while in one place stay
With sight so keen
They see their meal moving below
Thought unseen
This bird then dives
Silent, quick, the meal
Catches carries it away
Dines on the meal
Looks for another
From high in the sky
As the meal below
Far below moves by
While some birds soar or stand
Almost still in the air, diving-
Catching meals from there,
And fly.
Watch out...
Below.

A Lizard

I seen a little lizard
Small small like lizards be
I looked at the lizard
The lizard looked at me
I stood waved at the lizard
The lizard raised its head high
Croaked something in lizard
Looked walked into bushes
Slow away
I seen a little lizard
I seen a very interesting
Little lizard today.

Keen

So keen are the eyes of the hawk
As they fly others are seen
Tho they think they're unseen
And they're caught for the meal that the hawk
Flying sought
So keen are the eyes
Of the hawk.

Reddish Tint

Sunset with reddish tint
Of deep blue sky
Twilights gone evenings nigh
Dark replaces day
In silent quick of way
Lights appear as candles bright
In houses on streets
For it is night
Till dawn of day
As sunset with reddish tint
Of deep blue sky
Permits twilight leave
Evening, night come nigh,

Sings

The birds are so happy
In the mornings
They sing they sing they sing
And the world just seems
To listen
As each bird joyfully
Sings.

Winds

The light light winds
Of afternoon
Blew morning soft away
And afternoon came
Unnoticed till
Much later…
In the day.

Silence

Night time fell
And broke the silence
Of the light of day
And the silence stayed
Thru night till the light
Of day time day
Then the silence came
With dawn when the dawn… again
Lights night
Silence is free, silence has a way.

The Now

You only know of the now
You never know for certain
What the future has
For your plans
Of now
And may never know
Till the future appears
For sure
For you to know
If
You move the show
You only know of the now.

Crows

That crow, that crow
Up in that tree
Just hangs around
And wants the food
That's on the ground
And wants the food
That's on the table too
If we don't watch close
Very close
That crow and all its friends
They'll come, that's what
Just what, they'll do
They'll eat of the food
Those crows can find
Crows like to do that
Crow's they do
They do that all… the time

Stick

Roses are pretty flowers
They look nice
Smell nice and will stick you
When you touch them
You must be careful when you do.

Courage

It takes courage
The battle
To fight
It takes courage
The fire to fight
It takes courage sometime
To face the darkness
And the light
It takes courage at times…
The quiet to fight
It takes courage, the courage
That comes to each as detected
And flows individually
Silently
Thru the days
And lives
Lives on and on and on
Its way beautifully
Courageously
Day by day, just lovely
Day.

Passes By

Its about noon and now
The sunshine has come today
I thought the sunshine
Might not come today
But the sunshine has come
I think its whispering to the
Clouds of white in the sky
To move away let the blue
Of the heavens shine thru
For I see shadows of clouds
On the hill sides of clouds
Moving a side in the sky
For blue of the sky to come thru
Its about noon and now
Its whispering I think
To clouds of white
In the sky
To move drift silent in the sky
Make shadows on hillsides
Let blue of the heavens
Shine thru
While this beautiful day passes by.

Grass

When it rains
In the spring on green, green
Grass
The grass smells
Real nice
When you
Walk on the grass.
When it rains.

Fruit

Kiwi's are good
They smell good too
I know of
No other fruit
That smells like kiwi's do.

The Things

As we get older live alone
And do the things that we must do
Things take about a different hue
They stay or seem to move
About at times in ways
That appear at times
In ways they're really
Not supposed to but yet they do
Or at times one imagines that they do
Like rolling, touching, making noises
Moving about
Or perhaps its just
Ones imagination
Or maybe
Something there about
Anyway it helps to keep one on their toes
And serves to help keep
One on their toes
And serves to help keep
Life interesting as one
Goes about the days that go
As we get older live alone
And do the things that we
Must do.

The World

Of long ago it came to me
To see the world to feel the world
To hear the world
Quite differently
I understood then the way
The days the creator
Gave to each, each one
To choose the way
They felt each day
To them that comes
And gave them too
A holy book to read
And guide each thru
With pride
And use this book, each one
Can choose to or not to do
To help them thru
it matters not how big or small
The difficulties they may be
This Holy Book, its information too
Form the creator and true faith
Guides thru
Of long ago this came to me
And of all this
I'm sure you know
That the love of the creator
Is with you always
Thru faith and
Also.. In-
Eternal love
Where ere,
You go.

Apples

Apples look beautiful
On trees
And
Fresh apples
Smell nice
To me.

A Service

I went to my friends
Funeral service
But my friend
He was not there
His one son kept the ashes
Kept them
Somewhere, elsewhere
And at
My friends funeral service
When I went to the service
my friend
He was not there
Strange, strange
To miss your funeral service
Your funeral service
How strange.

Take Care

When things get rough
And life gets tough
Take care of yourself
Take care of yourself
Get proper sleep, get proper to eat
Learn to say yes, when
This is best
Learn to say no, when
This must be so
Be yourself be when this must be
Keep clean, get rest
Meditate some, pray much
Converse with friends
Be kind without end-
Honest too, yourself and,
Others too. Take care-
You'll make it thru, the days...in-
More enjoyable ways.

A System

Have a system
To do what you must do
That way
You can do
What you must do
And get thru it... if you
Have a system
To do what
You must do.

Little Town

Horses, wagons, and buggies
Oxen, ox carts too
A few tho not many folks
Had cars
In the little town
Of Peacock Michigan
Where I did grow
Many many years ago
The old steam train
Freight train, passenger train
Would go by about
Twice a day
Sometime stop on its way
Going by
There was a pickle station
When people raised
Cucumbers
In cucumber season
To make a little money
When growin weather
Was Sunny
There were two stores
In the little town
A one room school house
With grades from kindergarten thru 8th grade
About maybe 35 to 40 people
In the little town
Not many people around
Of course they're all gone now
Even the railroad track
Horses wagons, oxen
Ox carts
Old cars too
I guess
Just as time
Passes thru
That time, that kind
Of life
Passed too

Rain

It rained so much today
The flowers came out
The leaves on trees came out
The grass came too
To see what the rain
Was all about
And they all stayed
They liked the
Rain
When it rained today.

A Beautiful Day

Commitment to others
Has a lasting effect
Is a beautiful way
Everyday of
Expressing care
Love in a
Spiritual way
Thru care hope
Faith
Also commitment to others
Has a lasting effect
Of producing love
A special love
In
Beautiful ways.

Birds

The birds all came
To check and see
What I have left
For them
That's free.

Charm

The house when the children
Are raised and gone
Much of the house charm
They take along
Then when one spouse
Is lost with time
The house then becomes
Another kind
It becomes and is too
For only the home of
One
Kind of similar to
A turtles shell
Which still serves well
But quite similar to
An old shoebox
Filled with memories
The house where children
Are raised and gone
Then one spouse with time moves on.
Much charm of the
House is gone.
Memories tho are
Plentiful and... they flow with one
As lovely rivers, thru.

A Day

The house where a woman stays
Adds much to the life
Of a day
For there, things
Are arranged
In a much much different way
Than the way they're arranged
By a man
The dishes, the tables
The chairs, everything
Is arranged
By a woman's plan
That suits the house
In a woman's way
That makes it
To be
A family plan
The house where a woman stays
Add much to
The life of a day.

Used to Be

If pictures were there
Of what used to be
How wonderful, wonderful
That would be
But cameras few
Or none, then
Were to be
So only thoughts
And of memory
Then were to be
And that of now
Is of then
What we see-and hear,
Of most
Of what...used to be

Found Underground the Miners

The eyes of the world
Shine on you
From where you've been
For what you've done
Stayed away from
The world underground
Deep, deep underground
With no light around
For days and days
Almost 18 days
With no outside sounds
And no light around
With friends of many
All deep so deep
Underneath the ground
Near...far way
Then you were found
Thru love which is strong
Thru love which is felt
From about also deep
Deep and thru out
Everywhere around
And is felt in creation
Of the all. Silent very
Silent never, ever, leaves
Where ere one goes is
Always around. Found you with
All others and friends
Above
Friends below
With love thru love
Found a way thru love
With creations guidance too
To let you know
That everywhere the
Eyes of the world and
Love thru love, family
Love and all never
Forgot tho you were
Away far far away
Deep, deep under the earth
For days and days, 68 days

continued

A way was found
Thru creations love
To contact you
Bring light
Bring need, bring love
Bring you, back to above-with those
To those you love
Oh yes,
The eyes of the world
Shine on you
With heavens light
Like the sun, moon
Stars above
With eternal
Lovely love.

The Trail

Walk the trail
Thru the trees
Follow the path
Where it leads
Thru the trees
And green of grass
Walk the trail
See where the nature grows
Nature's path
Walk the trail, follow the path
Where it leads
Study the path. Walk on, walk thru.

Picnic

Have a picnic
Fill the park
Everybody come
Invite the birds too
To fly in, eat meander
And fly thru
When the parties over
Picnics thru
Empty the park
Everybody leave
Tell the birds
To fly out too
No more picnic
Close the parks
Everybody's thru

Go

When you're in your eighties
Seems like almost
Everywhere you go
Your very, very fast
Is most peoples slow
Still that's ok if
You're there when
They say go
And
You go
And go, go, go
You'll get there too
Tho
Maybe a little slow
When you're in your eighties
And you go.

Quiet

The earth gets real quiet
Right before twilight
Slips in
Then dark comes in
Thru the open gate
That stays open real late
Till dawn slides
Thru then closes the gate
Soon daylights
Here
And... till twilights quiet, then
It can hear, sense or feel
Right before dark
Appears really
Clear the - soft quiet,
Sounds of, evening and night...again.

We Forget

Sometime we forget
I can't really say
Say why
We forget to maybe
Lie on perhaps
Soft grassy hillsides,
And just look up at
The free lovely
Beautiful sky
Up so very very high
Sometime we forget
I can't really say why tho
But we forget to
Look up and enjoy
The wide open sky.

Friendly

Picnicking, having a party
With children , friends
Families, family style
Too… on a nice day
That's friendly and
Fun too
At a nice park
Sometime
Is a fun thing to do
Try it sometime
You might like it
Too.

Cloudy Today

It's cloudy, its cloudy
Real cloudy today
The sky is blue
But clouds hide it
Away
An airplane
I hear flying
Way over the clouds
High in the sky
Where the sky is all blue
But I cannot see it
Cloudy hides it away
The sun it is shining
High up in the sky all
Where the sky is blue
Its hazy, hazy, hazy
Here today
Clouds hide
The sun away
Its cloudy too, its cloudy
Real cloudy today
And maybe it will
Be cloudy for
The rest of the day.

It's Cool

It's cool, it's cool
It's real cool
And
Kind of windy today
The birds, only a few
Are flying today
It must be cool
In the air
To the birds
When they fly today
Of course
I don't know
I cant fly anyway
But I know
It's cool, it's cool
And
Kind of windy too, today.

Special Tree

Theres a special tree
Means much to me
A tree growing green
With multi colored leaves
Of red and green
That tree was planted for
And in memory too-
Twas for, is for, my wife,
My family, and for me too
There's a special tree
That will always mean
Very much to me.

Bang

When firecrackers
go bang
And are thru
I don't like
The powder smell
Do you?

People Go

People, people they must go
To places
Where they want to go
I've ridden in buses
And in auto cars too
That use gasoline
To make them go
Taking people places
Where they want to go
And in Japan when
I was young about 18 or so
More than 60 years ago I rode in buses
Taxis auto cars
Using gases
From coke wood fire
To make
The engines go
Taking people to places
Where they want to go
People must go, go, go
To places
Where they want to go

One Another

To love one another
As creations created
Not as war or politics
Has brought about
Is the only way
The worlds can become
Related
And be peaceful all
Throughout
Is to
Love one another
As the creator created
Not as war misunderstanding
Or politics
Has brought about

For Helping

Thanks for helping
In ways you
didn't even know
Help to those
Who need help
Speaks silent
Speaks low
Thanks for helping
In ways
You didn't even know
It's golden
It's lovely
Much appreciated
Eternal too
Thanks,
Thank you

As We Go

We graduate
As we go
From one day
To another day
And we diminish
Or we grow
In our own
But silent way
As we go
From one day
To another day
We do this
On our own
This big individual
Very personal, silent
Graduation
A self administered event
Of knowledge
Lost or gained, regardless of age
As we graduate
As we go
Form one day, to another day

Day

The day will have to
go away
For night is coming
With dark
To cover where day
Has been
The day will have
To go away
For night with dark
Is with silent
Moving in
A sky of night I see
With a blue of mystery
Dark, for night is here
Day is done.

Beautiful

It's really quite beautiful
To watch the sky
Right before daylight
Is nigh
How the moon disappears
From the sky
The stars still shine
Bright in the sky
The dark slowly disappears
From the sky
The sunlight starts
To brighten up the sky
Quite bright, quite beautiful
Too
Right before and while daylight
Is coming thru
It's really, really beautiful
To watch the sky
Right before daylight is nigh.

Country Stream

Just listen to that beautiful little
Cool clear water gossipy
Country stream
Running thru
The country side
Gurgling, gossiping
To the summers green grass
Trees, leaves
Sunny blue sky
And everything
Just listen to that
Beautiful little
gossiping stream
Isn't it beautiful?

I'll Remember

Last night was the visit, when you came
I'll remember, I'll remember
For a long long time
It was different not as times
Before not the same
For it seemed I was
Nearly awake but not quite
But understanding feeling
The feeling of touch and such
For I remember feeling
When I reached to touch you
Where you always laid
For the many, many years
I felt your knee
There you be
And in my mind
Of half awake, half asleep
At the time.
I could feel this is real
Then I think our hands
Touched, my mind then
Thought this is not
A dream, this could not be
This is real
I then remember speaking to you a little of
Our talking I remember
I do remember
Asking you, you are
Here with me and you said yes
I am here
You said something else
I can't remember that but I remember
Asking you
Is it cold where you are
About where you were
Then I remember but it was an answer
Slightly errie not
Something you normally say
Then I remember you
Moved to climb over me
In what I thought to be an embrace
Of love
I could feel your body travel

continued

Continues… I'll Remember

If from dream perhaps it twas
For I was half asleep
Half awake, love I'm sure
It was there for many
Years we were in love
But after that I awoke
In full I awoke
I looked over where you would lay
The sun was bright
It was day, you were
Not there you were away
I will never forget, were you there
Had you in some way been there?
Was it my imagination
I could feel your touch
I remembered all the time
You were with our creator
I remembered this in
My mind my state of mind
At the time
Still this event
This dream whatever
It came to be
It seemed real, quite real
Not before the same
To me
I'll remember , I'll remember
Last night the visit when you came
It seemed you would
Remain but with day
You were away
Your stay was lovely
Come anytime, night or day
Our years, our 58 years together
Were lovely,
Love has its way.

Was Spring

And it was spring
Breezes blew
Love grew
Soft winds and love
Was all about
Blossoms came to trees of green
Filled valleys
Hills and dales, extreme-
While flowers
Grew with beauty
all round
At nights silvered moonlight rays
With silent lovely
Appeared
For it was spring
Breezes soft beautiful
Blew
And silently love
Lovely simply lovely
Was felt thru birth
A wonder
In the spring of new,
Of new life…
And, it was spring.

Enemies

Of all the enemies
I can see
The worst… I think….
Is, me.

To Do

So many things
To choose from
So many things
To do
I can't be me
I can't be you
I'll just be
Somebody new
So many ,many-
Things to do, to choose from
Too
I don't know what
To do.

A Shadow

I seen a shadow
Passing
And it came
From in the sky
I think it was from a bird
That was flying in the sky
Flying by not too high
Maybe the bird
Seen its shadow on the ground
And it flew low
And all around
Then it flew off
High up
And into the sky
That's why I think
I seen a shadow
Passing
And it came from the sky.

Paints

They are mixing paints
On hard pieces of paper
The children are
Mixing paints on pieces of paper
And colors of many different kind
Yellows with green
Reds with blue
All different colors
Just to name a few
And the colors that come
Will really surprise you
The children really
Enjoy what they do
Are doing too
Very good painters
The children are
For paintings like these
The parents will be surely proud
Like may be they owned
A beautiful drifting cloud
Or maybe the morning star.
Or perhaps a flying
Carpet
From a famous
Distant country
Far off really
Really far
But the paintings
Were made by
The children their children
Mixing paints
Their way
Many colors of paints today.

To Do Something

Sometime when it's
Possible too
It's really good to do something
You haven't really done
For years like
Hammer things, drill, sand metal
Fashion make, cut use screws
Nuts, bolts, construct something
If it's something useful it's
Even better
Today I constructed a push broom
With a broken metal handle
So I t could be once more
Attached to the broom
With a self made attachment
It had been laying around
For years
Good project it was very
Successful
Took 2 or 3 hours
Sometime when it's possible too
It really good to do something
You haven't done for years
Especially if you're over
80 years old, feels good too.

Scream

To listen,
While others holler
And scream over things of small
With little matter
To be silent
And speak with love
As clouds above
Where sunlight stays
Is quite all right
And more that matters
Also is,
A better way.

Theirs

Shovels move dirt
Wheels more items
Good items moved
In honest
Produce honest work
Work honest work
With love which
Builds solid the forever
As shovels
Move the dirt and
Wheels roll on
With honesty only
On
Creating a future
A chosen future
For each daily their way
Slowly each day lovely or
Sunny cloudy shoveling wheeling
Theirs with memories of and
For them, thru the then,
On and on and on.

Way's

The awakening of dawn
The swift coming – of noon
The quaint slip in of twilight
The tip toe ishness – in of evening.
The permanence of dark-
And coming of night, all have an effect on
Something each day as they –come and go
Each … in their soft, silent of way's.

Varying Memories

With another
Close but far, alone almost
Were the two thru
The years
And separated slightly
As stars on high
While years went by
Then storms came, sunshine
More storms relentless, changing
Almost unbearable at times
Assistance form storms
Most family storms
Not around available or complete
Not any where around
Permanent
To be found
One violent storm
Complete4ly destroyed
One of the two
While memories flow at times
For the other of two
Remaining alone close but far
Separated by far
As stars on high above
That drift with
Varying memories
Of love, drift
In silent by.
Like unknown
Open space, in-
Open sky.

To See

A planetarium
If never you
One did see
Is something to go
And see, there
You can see
How they
The planets, stars
Sun, moon, constellations
Small large star dippers
Milky way many
Things in the heavens
Above will be
A planetarium is
Something nice to see
We took many children to see
A planetarium today
A Planetarium is,
Nice to see.

Wherever

My house, my house
Wherever it be
Is
My house, my house
And is there
In its
Entirety
Forever
And
Will always be
My house, my house
Forever,
Whatever it be.

Be

Real, real young
Most don't know
Just when they be
Halfway thru
Maybe some
Start to see
And prepare
For whom they
Really are and want
Most to be
But real real
Young
Most don't really
Know just
When, they be.

Our Lives

The times of our lives
We have them
They're given to us
And when we have them
We hardly know
That we have them till
They're finished and gone
Then we think long long after
Those were the times
the times of our lives
And we had them
We had them
They were
Given to us
Then
The times of our lives
The times of our lives
Thanks, thanks
They were eternally marvelous.

Something

Everybody's got
Something that bugs them
Some little smirk
Or quirk
Something they like or dislike
Love
Or hate like
Or can hardly take
That maybe is what
Really helps keep us
Going to keep doing better
Less or what it takes
Seems when we admit
Everybody's got
Something that
Bugs them
Some little smirk
Or quirk, we better... make it thru.

.

Musical Note

The faint distant strains
Of a soft musical note
Or song to life as it flows
Oh so very softly by
Are hardly visible
But visible to the
Naked eye or ear
Felt by the hand
And seen in the
Footprints
Faint of time
Sublime oh so
Sublime, heard
In a musical breath
As soft distant strain
To life as it flows
Oh so very softly, by– is,
Lovely and ... appreciated.
Also connects
A something, as all
Flows so permanently,
By.

Flowers

Little children's fingers
Pick the flowers
Of spring time in
spring time days
Then grow as flowers
Day by day
Children flowers
Day and hours
Little fingers picking
Spring time flowers
Growing growing
Thru the hours
Thru the seasons
Little children
Little children
And the flowers growing.

Wonderful

So beautiful
So lovely
So simply wonderful
Too
To have a birthday
With family
And loved ones too, seems
You are blessed its beautiful, Eternally
Wonderful thru
Creation and
With love filled
With love for you.
Beautiful, lovely,
Simply, so...wonderful too.

The Fog

Like smoke like smoke
The fog it comes
For some it seems
Quite bothersome
But for most
It comes
Then goes away
To come again
Another day.

Toes

Walking running
As you go sometime
You stub your great big toe
Cause it hits the ground first
As you move around
If it hits and scrapes
The ground and tears
The skin as you move around
It lets you know
It hurts and bleeds right then
In its way it lets you know
You feel it say
Loud really loud
And in its way , say
Hey, hey, hey
Walking running as you go
Pick up your toes
Your great big toes
We don't like it when you hurt us
As you walk
And run around

Far Away

I'm going down
To the ocean today
Where I can look
Out to
Far far away
And see where the ocean
And sky meet
Their way
Where the water birds soar
Where the sun shines free
Where no buildings be
And only trees and plants
And other things be
On its outer proximity
Permanently
I'm going down to
The ocean today
Where I can look out
Only temporarily
To and feel of the
Far, far, away.
I'm going down
To the ocean,
Today.

Away

Hurry, hurry with the day
Its passing rapidly away
Twilight comes
Only stays brief
To welcome night
And night passes, passes
With leisure thru
But
Hurry, hurry with the day
For it
It passes rapidly away.

Rush

Sometime,
When you rush, rush, rush
Getting things to
Take with you
You walk right by
And leave some of the things
You just rush, rush, rushed
To take with you.
And when you get back
The things are waiting,
Wondering why
You didn't say goodbye
When you, rush, rush, rushed
Going by, not always- but
This happens, sometime.

Today

I thought the sun
Would never shine
But there it shines
Today
I thought the clouds
Would never go away,
But there's blue
In the sky today
At times our thoughts
Can be amiss
When sunshine
Lights the day
And light shines thru
Form up above
With love
Like it does
Today

Bye

Moonlight, moonlight
Starlight too
Light the sky
Till day
Comes thru
Then sunlight, sunlight
Light the sky
Till evening comes
And …
Starlight, moonlight
Tell sunlight,
Bye.

Quiet

Slow, soft, quiet music
In a way
Soothes
Like a rippling
Mountain stream ,
Brings carries
Water away.
Slow, soft, quiet music
In a way...soothes,
Its way.

31

Journey

The journey of life
Takes us along
To places we would
Maybe never go
Except to perhaps
Sing of, in song
But life is
Generous it takes
Us along
For when life
Moves its way
We have no say
The journey of life
Takes us along
We must adapt
As we go
And sing the new
Song as
Life takes us along
Thru and
To the new...of life.

Speaks

Jazz music
With a sax
And piano
Speaks with no words
Thru music
Its way
A silent
Yet
In a musical
Way.
Chords of music
Nicely
Played
On guitar strings
Are nice
To listen To, cause-
Music charms, improvises,
The soul,
Wordlessly.

Shines

The sunshine fades
The moon does too
But shine again
When their time comes too
And with love
They shine
Tho sunshine fades
And moon does too
Their love shines
Mysteriously
Lovely thru.

Things

Scissors and things
In surgery
Rooms
With no windows
To look thru
Are kind of like
Space
Your mind sees thru
Momentarily
While your mind there views
Those scissors and things
You leave this
Room soon– if,
Possible.

Thoughts

Maybe 4 or 5 months ago
I started taking airplane
Flying lessons at the
Salinas airport here in town
And found its a nice kind of
Way to pass stress
Built up in and with days
Away with time as you go
Seems like time spent
Up there high and away
Slips by with clouds
That float free by
And thoughts especially
Ones not needed when
Back on earth again
Remained somewhere
A loft on high winds
That soar the heavens
High.
And one is free to
Fill the mind with
Other thoughts
And again move free
Like birds that fly
Who knows their thoughts
Or where they store
Them when a loft...and-
As I write these words,
My thoughts they change
In day in night especially
When midnight is passed
And on its way.
The night gets long
As long as day or more

Continued

And when the mind seems
Filled. To fly up
Soar with high the
Clouds is beautiful
And leave some thoughts
While between the
Heavens yes the earth
Leave some there with a
Sky of blue and land
Again feel somewhat
As new.
This thought I leave
At close of day.
Do what is good
Do while you may.
For days they go
They fly –
And come again
They stay, while
You – you...
Fly away.

Good Day

Start the week off in a way
That usually makes for a pretty good day
Go to where folks gather to be
Where they can worshipping- be free.
You can find good there if you do
That is...if you really, really, want to- and start
The week off in a way that usually makes for
A pretty good day.

Up

Just keep on looking up
Looking up – looking up
Even tho the clouds
Are there
There's sunshine
Always there
Right over the clouds
Its there
Its always
There
No matter where
You are
Sunshine somewhere
Is there – if –
You look hard
You will find
Sunshine sunshine
You'll find
Never ever look back
Or behind
Look up-on forward
And thru
You'll find
Sunshine
And love,
You'll find – a way
And thru.

Nothing

With nothing to do
Find something to do
Or you soon , may do-
Just… nothing.

Slip Slide

Sometime in the evening
When its quiet
When its still
When in the evening
That of day
That of twilight
Of night too – mix
Will
And at one time
Deep in the mind
Come faintly thru
As if in haze
And appear like
If a cloud – then
Reappear
In mind as should
Then slip and mix
Some way and cause –
And make a memory
This causes one
To pause and think
What now just what
Is this and what
Or why does is this
And why just why
Does this kind of
Thinking be
Or will or will it not
Just pass – with time
Sometime I holler
Yes sometime that I do
And then it – and I
Slip slide in a way
Slide bump, into another day.
Happens tho,
Sometime.

Transport

Most pictures are really
Nice to see
only one picture tho
That special picture
Can transport
Quickly
One
To its
Reality.
Of– where...
Only that,
Person, knows
That picture-
That ... only-
Picture.

Little Bit

Put
A little bit here
Put
A little bit there
Put
A little bit in
The food
A little everywhere
It
Makes everything nice
Everything smooth
Everyone likes it
People fight
Some
Not tho everyone
Population goes down
That's why we do it
And now
You got it
And bye.

The Tree

Big crow, big crow
Why are you in that tree?
Why are you in that tree?
Because the tree
Because the tree
Because the tree was here
For me
That's why I the crow
Am in the tree
The tree, the tree
Was here for me.

Away

A room without windows
Only doors
Implores
There you be
Here you are
Away
And far
From reality.

Pile

When things just seem to
Pile and pile and pile
They push you in a corner
It seems
You cant see over
The pile
You cant see around
The pile
You cant but see
The pile
You cant see under
The pile
Just get away for awhile
Think of another way
For awhile
Rest see a little day
For awhile
Then come back and attack
Another way
Relax for awhile.
Soon…
Piles somehow
Are not piles anymore
They're just
Another days chores
So when things just
Pile, pile, pile relax awhile
Do something else awhile
Then attack the pile again
Piles usually get
Smaller
And they seem to
go away
Making life a
Better day.

Tomorrows

Children accomplish,
Our dreams
of tomorrows
Sometime-childishly.

Time

The clocks have a way
Of giving us something
Which gives us thru
Seconds and minutes
Hours we can see on
A dial and count
Also sunshine evening
Night season
Give a reason to count
This too
And it's time
Which is and can be too
Kind, lovely, it always
Tho… creates memories
Of choice seemingly
For its there
By the creator
Same for all then
Changed some by
Creation but most
By individual choice
To be this time
Times for lovely kind
Nice or like… ice if chosen,
Thru
The seconds, minutes
Hours, years, days
Also has it seems ways
Of blending quiet
Silent, yet permanent
In each individuals
Memories, desires
Dreams
This world, this world
Of… time.

Sometimes

Dislike sometimes
Needs better
Acquaintance
Of… dislike, creating like.
The two– with time– this
Can do, sometime.

The Memory

The memory of
A love lost
Will last forever, special ways
I'm sure it will return
As the seasons time to time
Will be relished when it does
In ways known only
To the loved one
For those who left
Speak it seems instantly
When called
And converse lengthy
When called upon
In manner completely understood
Some may say this cannot be
Some may say this is impossible
But only those
Who have traveled this highway
Know of this– each,
Travels on their own and
Respond in various ways
Speak to others who have been
This way before
They will respond much in this way
Each has memories much the same
In different ways
Of a spouse of any years lost
And memories they return
In many ways for years and years
Forever days in loving ways– sometime.

Sends and Gives

These poems
These poems
They come to me
I write them down
Then I can see
All can see
These poems, these poems
That come to me
It seems from everywhere
The birds in air
The clouds the skies and
Even little butterflies
The things that move
And things that don't
Can't even move
Or simply won't
The sunlight, clouds
Starlight, moonlight
Oh, the lovely
Haunting moonlight
I think its just
Lovely quiet and
So silent
Moving thru
Then there's the
Rain, soft, stormy
Helpful, life giving
Too
I watch it
Write of it
As it moves some days
Fascinating it is
It has fascinating ways
All this and much more too
These poems, these poems
Are filled with this
And much, much, more
As the creator
Whom I thank
Sends and gives
Them to share
To share
With others, and
With me...These poems.

Many Years

Had not seen you
For many, many years
Since I left town
As a teenager
When you were around
I seen you this morning
In a dream you were
In a choir with me
Partially but partially
As old very old
From underground
I remember you too
When my father made
A yoke of wood for a
Team of oxen for you
I was maybe of age
10 years plus two
And you then of age
Maybe 68 years plus two
Now in the mouths
Of about two
I will be age
Years eighty and three
Yet I had a dream
Of you in a choir
There with me
And I had not seen you
Since I left a small
Small town as a teenage
When you were around
Tho you were there it
Seemed you were partially
Underground
Also after the dream
Information came to my mind
Of very special kind
That helps to solve
Tremendously
A problem that had been
Bothering me

continued

Continues… Many Years

And I remember now
Of talking to you
As a child of problems
I then, was growing thru
My parents and you
Solved problems then
In that wee small town
In Michigan
And now a problem
solved
Today
Dreams, dreams, dreams
Seem to flow silently
Beautifully thru life
Cycling, cycling their way,..
During slumber.
Thru, the years.

The Ages

Down thru the ages
My ages to me
I see all of
The things
I be to me
These things I see
Some I like some
I don't like
But
These things I see
Down thru the ages
My ages
To me.

Enjoy

Big moon tonight
All pretty and full
Blue sky tonight
With moon, stars, and their mystery
Filled.
Enjoy tonight
While it
Passes thru
With its big moon...
Blue sky
Star filled, and -
Mystery too.

The Morning

Early in the morning
While I was camping
Form a hill near
Far away
I seen lights of
A town
Only me, was around
And the town far away
It was friendly
To see
Seen by only me
For me
Tho those in the town
Knew not of me
But I did see, in the morning
A town early and
The lights of a town
Early in the morning
While I was camping
From a hill of near
Far sway.

An Afternoon

Enjoying music
In a restaurant-an,
eatery, eating too
On a Sunday afternoon
Is a
Quiet relaxing way
After the hour of two
Before the hour of three
At least for me
Slips slow, slow
Slowly, lovely
Just eating light
Enjoying music
Kind of
Slips a
Sunday afternoon
Quietly, lightly
Toward
Evenings twilight
In a quaint
Kind of way
Silently.

A Song

Life itself has a way
Kind of similar
To the notes of a song
And we must move
With the song
As we flow with the days
For the best
Tune we can hear
As we move thru
For
Life itself has its way
Kind of like the
Notes of a song.

Houses

A house I have
A house I have
Worth thousands of dollars
And more
But it's nice
To go camping
go camping sometime
And be where I now be
With just the ground
the floor
Many around me here I think
Think same
For they come every day
From houses
Camping
More and more
Day by day
More , more
From far away.

Windy Sky

A bird in a windy sky
Hardly move it's wings
Passing by
The bird flies with the wind
And the bird and the wind
Play, playfully
In the windy sky.

Wind

It's windy here today
No one I know
Has ever seen the wind
Do you think, if you could
See the wind
You would like the wind?
If I could see the wind
I'm pretty sure I would like wind
It's windy here today

Really do

Try it, try it and
Say you might like it
I know I do
I really really do
It's a day of
All your own
You don't do anything
But that what you
Want to do that you
Really want to do
That's good to do
Try it its relaxing
It really really is
Kind of lets you in a way
Kind of catch up with the world
And you
Try it try it and
Say you might like it
I know I do I really, really do

Clouds

Clouds in the sky
Blue sky too
It's a windy day
Nice day too
Just a nice windy day
Passing thru.

This Way

In the dark of the moonlight
That's where what's left
Of daylight stays
Twas there it went when
Twilight to evening
Tucked daylight away
And that's where it
Will stay
Till dawn sends moonlight
And night
On their way
Then daylight from
Dark of moonlight
Will come again
This way.

Hawk

Today is windy
I'm camping today
And from today's windy
Late evening sky
I'm watching a large bird
A hawk flying slow
Quiet in the sky
Searching below perhaps
For an evening meal
From the sky
Watch out little animals
On the ground below
The hawk flying slow quiet
In the sky may
See and catch you
For its evening meal
From they sky.

She

So much strong drink
To drink did she
She did not know
Just who she be
Then she doeth something bad
Did she
The police taketh her away
To bring her back
Another day when
She knows better, just who she be
Where
Camping, drinking, this did she
Poor she, to she.

Camped

I looked up at the moon
Where I camped in the night
All round and yellow
Shining lovely over the valley
With the stars
Beautifully
In dim dark light
And the house lights
In my early morning view
caused the view to be
Everlasting to me
The valley the moon
The stars
The moonlight, I'll forever
Remember blended together
As I looked
Up at the moon
Where I camped in the night.

Graceful

The hawk so graceful
In the sky does fly
Observing its movements
In the sky
Seems to cause
Seconds
To go slow
by.
So quiet, lovely too,
Thru.

Low

The moon is now low
In the sky just waiting
And
When dawn appears
The moon will soon
Then
Disappear
From the sky.
Till night,
The moon– its
Just waiting.

A Disagreement

I watched a disagreement
Today in the sky
Between two crows and
A soaring hawk
Pecking him repeatedly
Driving the hawk far far away
Then the two crows returned
The hawk did not return
At that time
Today when
I watched a disagreement
Today in the sky.

Watch

Birds watch as they fly
In the sky
Friends and foes
As they fly
So gracefully by.
In and, thru the sky.

That is True

Just what makes the wind to blow
Do you think we'll ever know
Just what makes a seed grow
Do you think we'll ever know
Just what makes the ocean so deep
Or what makes sky so high
Or what keeps the sun so bright
Or what keeps the stars
And sun and moon
In orbit for years and years
And centuries too
All this and even more
What gives a life
And keeps it too
Then takes it back
When life is thru
If all this we know
With it what could we do
Perhaps teach it to others
In lovely ways
For true love
Helps bring more love thru
That we know is true.

Viewing

Viewing the moon tonight
Round full with its
Yellowish glow
Mid deep darkish blue
Of the heavens
Star filled glow
While standing on
The hillside of a valley below
homes of few and many
With lights of few
In an early morning
Too
And in valley of dark
Still of midnight glow
Gave a feeling of
Wondrous ;lovely
Eternal
And an almost maybe
Unexplainable view of it
Too while viewing
The moon tonight.

Hi

I was camping and
I waved at a crow
Flying by
The crow looked and
didn't even say
Hi
Then I reminded myself
Hey
You just told a crow
Hi
And I say why?
Try it sometime
Even
If you're not camping

Heart of the Moon

The heart of the moon
That must be where
The beauty comes form
When the moon is bright
And full
With lovely mysterious
Moonlight
Just shining soft
All around everywhere
Magic, in the night
From the moon, stars, and heavens
Or maybe the very
Heart of the moon
Is from
Where that silent
Lovely light
The soft, soft
Moonlight comes.

Away

The night I think
Absorbed the evening
Which took the twilight
And day
Tho the dawn
The nights new friend
Promises to bring day
Soon
Twill be good
To see day
Since twilight
And evening
Took it away.

To View

As I look at you
As the days pass thru
The more of you
Comes thru to view
As the days have ways
To make years and seasons
Their way
And folks live on
And say live on
And you are you
And I am I
And they are they
And you don't know me
And I don't know you
While think
Maybe
I know of you
Bits of you
Maybe
While passing thru
Just passing thru to view.
Up is up
And
Down is down
Been that way
Since I been
Around
Maybe what we view in
Our minds at times is
Memories of what has before
Been
Now that could be too for
Memories have before been
Have to have been to be
A memory how about that.

A Passin Thru

My cat, my cat
We've passed quite a few years
Years together
My wife, my cat, and I've
Been thru
My wife left a few years ago
Now the cat and I
Are here together
She stays in the garage
And outside
And is naturally a getting
Older so am I
As we here abide
She and I both are
Are a taken on ways
As we here do stride
Lately where we collide
Cat and people ways
Where we don't
Get along
Together
Cats ways peoples way's
Getting so she don't
Want to go outside
Or is getting
Afraid to or something
And is making the garage
Dirty inside
Now that can't be
That just can't be
I can't talk cat
She can't talk people
We have to get along
Best way were able
That cat with my wife and I
We've been together for quite
A few years
Have to keep that in mind too
Were a travelin this road thru
Together

continued

In our way, our time
Our times
With time must keep
That in mind
Tho its hard to do
Sometime
got to do that tho
All the time
Keep it together, peaceful
Ways as we
Pass thru together
Nights and days
Together a passin
Thru
Just a passin
Thru– She's a cat, and
I be people
That's me.

Lightly

The light – with dawn thru morning
Say's nothing- in it's way
But speaks, like thunder to you
With great respect,
All thru the day soft- lightly…
That's it's way. The light.

Faith

When there's been-
Two in the house
And one's gone away
To stay forever
It changes the day
It changes the night
It changes things
Most everything
In a way
Specially if its
A spouse.
That's been there for years
Most like a body-
To lose sound giving ears.
To not have the sound
That's been always around.
When at night and
Sun giving light changes
Quiet like to dark giving
Night. The day changes
To quiet lonesome
Of night and when
One is alone
With only quiet as friend
As strangeness lurks there
That's always been there
But of very low key
When spouse mate
Right there be
To discuss loud or in
Silence life things
Eternally.
Oh yes – when there's
Been two in the house
And one's gone away
To stay forever
It changes the day
It changes the night
It changes most
Everything in an
Understanding very, very
Different, never before
Way.

Continued

Not the same as a child
Going away with both
Spouses for support
In the house.
But quite similar to
One in a storm with
No roof on a house
Where the storm with
No roof on a house
Where the storm is
Felt no matter where
You be with no roof
One can feel comfort
From or see.
Till the storm goes
Away and begins a
I think I truly think
And its heart felt
Thinking I now write
Of and from deep
Feeling – deep inside
That true feelings
Feelings – honest.
Talk from others
Even just closeness
Company of others
That's there with
Honesty offering company
Help in some way
Helps in some way
Helps tremendous
While one deals with
The change of the loss
Of a spouse and the
Love of a spouse
Which lives as the
Seasons slightly ever
Slightly but in its way
Thru memory forever

continued

Continues… Faith

But as the seasons
Can be changed thru
Sunshine, rainbows,
Mysterious moon light
Dawn noon's – twilight
All giving love, and
Love, only love –
I´m sure the spouse
Lost would give and
Creation will send
Tho gradual feelings
Of better and
Understanding – in
And with given time
For creation we
Must remember
Gave the precious
Gift of love thru
A lovely spouse and
Togetherness with
Love for a given time
So the creator will
Give healing thru
Trust and faith
And patience.
In given time.
Also give in love.
Eternally.
Have and –
Keep faith.

Doing

Been so busy
So very very busy
Doing things –
Good and bad
That I haven´t
Had time
To think of
What was really
Good or bad.
By doing everything
Keeping busy.
Really feeling
Pretty good
Maybe that
Is what one
Must do –
Keep busy – keep busy
And do what´s good
There is to do
And help everyone
Pull pull – the big
Load thru
That's what
I been doing
Working at school
With the kids
Working at church
With the choir and
Rummage sale
Pulling – pulling
The load
Doing ,doing, doing
What must be done
All the way
One can see
With everyone
Helping pull the load
Get it thru
Keeping busy
And with others
Doing what we think
Best
That we think is the best
To do.

Some Days

You know – somedays
Is good, some days
Seems like
What happened before
Maybe back in
The month of April
Seven months ago
Tries to come here
Now – where I'm going
And must go
To keep pace
With where that
I must be.
Doing the good and all
There is so –
I can be.
And find mixed
In a way – causing
The thinking to
To kind of feel
Happy to think
Back to the month
Of April and my
Spouse that had to leave
Went away
And the now
Thats with me now
But this comes
With memory
And comes and stays
Then goes away
And does the nights
As does the days
And life goes on
And thru it all
We something must
Remember
That where theres love
Eternal love
Thru out all days
Love covers
All.

For Free

Awake not asleep
And tired too
Almost asleep not awake
And tired too
Can mix with you
And neither be,
Safe nor sane
When it happens to you
Awake not asleep
And tired too
Almost asleep not awake
And tired too
These things of life
That sometime be,
And are for free.
Must be handled
Properly.

Waiting

Sit and think
And half the day
Just goes away
Then night time
Comes and morning too
Another day
Comes
Passing thru
To sit and think in
Waiting,
For you.

Today

The time now is –
Nearly nine – nine
Of night oh yes – that's right
The hours of night
Seems eating time for me
Since April when life
Changed, my spouse went away
Forever from me
And times are changing
But not completely
Today's been well – the
Weather was hot
Very hot for here
I think 90 or somewhere
Near.
In the morning I worked
At college with Pre-
School folks from 3 they be
To 4 thru 5 very alive.
Some painted
Some read some sang
Some made kites to fly
Some made bracelets
And necklaces
Whatever they came by
Most stopped and they talked,
Kept me busy this
Morning, till morning
Went by
I then ate lunch
In my car
In the cool parking
lot listened to the
Radio dozed there
For an hour or so.

Continued

Then drove home
Parked car in the garage
Conversed with my
cat rusty
Who climbed to top of,
It the car watching
All from high and
afar.
Where she listens
Sleeps snoozes, sleeps
Peaceful her day
Away.
I then repaired
Partially a light
A little each day
So my purchased job
From the rummage
Sale won't too
rapid go away.
Then I worked on
My children's story
Of Anthony the dragonfly
And Rudolph the humming
Bird their doings
Their travels all it
Could stir
And now I'm thinking
Bedtime
Since its almost
A quarter to ten
I'd best go eat
So today or what's
Left of today
Will be
A very well spent
But good day it,
Has been.

Mercy Me

It's 3:30 in the morning
And here I sit
Oh mercy me
Why ain't I in bed
Where I should be
In stead of sitting here
What's wrong with me
But at least
I'm aware that
In bed's where
I should be
At least the thoughts
Still there as
My company
And I'm on my
Way to bed
The place where,
I should be
But...
It's 3:30 Tuesday
Morning
Why ain't I in bed
Where I should be
Oh mercy,
Mercy me.

Feels

Love is not
What one sees
But where one
Feels within
That's where it lies.

Weather

Weather's usually to hot- or too cold
Finding perfect weather, pleasing all the time
Serves to make one old.
Weather's usually … take what comes-
And smiling, grow old.

Thru

As thoughts come
Then pass right thru
Of what there was
And still is to do
Of what we've done
Still think or
Want to do.
Seems all mixed
Or slightly so
Of where to start
The place to best
Push
And desired
Get thru.
To not get mixed
With past and now
And then to now
Then be in past
And now
Some how
That's good
That's bad
And easy too
At times we do
As we pause
As thought comes
Of past and now
As when they pass
With silence
Thru.

50

To Do

With two
Its more easy
At times, to do
What must be done
But with one
One still can do
With care
With caution too
And carry
Tremendous load
With care
Along the way
Each day
The path gets long
With only one
Shadow cast-tho
Far and near
And lone some
And dark in silence
Making silent
Thunderous sounds
Where two can
Discuss what ere
There be-and
In this way set
Silence free
One can this do
With caution too
But...
With two at times
Sometimes-all the time,
Its more easy to do.

Everyday

Work everyday in some way
To stop working in someway,
You soon- May…stop you.
So- work everyday,
In – someway.

Pulses

Noise-noise come
Then the quiet
Passes away
And I heard the noise
And blaring of the day
It was nice to hear
To my listening body
And my ear
The quiet was
Yet near
But the noise
My ear my body
Could hear
Or the pulses
Of the quiet
As the quiet
Passed its way
Mid blaring of the day… was-
Soothing in soft.

Leaves

Soft rustles
The wind
Leaves on the trees
Today –
I see leaves move
From the room,
Where I stay.
With
The wind.

Appointment

Have a 2:30pm
Appointment
With chiropractor
Today.
To see if he can help
A muscle left hip knee
Pain I acquired
Most while helping
My wife before
Get back or her body retain
Some of its agility
That it had before
Never went to one
Of these type healing
Places hope they're
Not like throwing
Water at the moon
Or like sweeping
With a left handed
Broom.
But soon I'll know
Cause...
Come what may
I have a 2:30pm
Appointment
With a chiropractor,
Today.

Since

Since you left now- over two years ago most
Only sounds in the house are those of mine
The rooms, they may have forgot sounds
Of others, cause... they hear only mine.
Our's tho, must be here somewhere too
From our 58 years together- and the two years ago
Since you left , in time.

A Greeting

A hello is a greeting
And a way to start
The day in a beautiful way
A handshake
And a smile too
Permeates thru
Mixing, communicating . leading
In many ways
Thru a world that
Gives beauty
Has hills, small, large
Mountains of tall
Far away close
Purple with laze
With clouds, sunshine too
And also a creation
With rainbows of
Colors lovely, and of
Sunshine, moonlight, starlight
Given freely with love
Having traveled thru
This creation
Witnessed the beauty
Climbed the mountains
Conquered
Waved a victory
Communicated – my way
Loved and raised a family
To friends and all, now
With my leaving
As of a sunset lovely
Consider – said my friend silently.
A hello to evening
And love – to sunrise.

Decisions

So many decisions
To make everyday
To do this - that
If this is good
That bad - or
Whether this should
Be done or that
If done is good
Or that bad or
Both needed – just fun
Or... if you're just
Getting old older
Maybe you're
Having your family
History retold.
Like today's – having
House cleaning
Decisions made
Is this needed
As decided upon
Or is it a goodie
That should a been
Not have been done
Or chiropractic visit
That you never –
Have done before,
That you done today
Could it have not
Be done – but…
You had it done
Was it, a
Could a – have not
Been done – but you
Had it done – was it
Another, could a
Would a have not
Been done that you
Had it done or not

Continued

continues ...Decisions

These decisions
You do that you think
You must do
Maybe... they're
Good for you
Because –
They keep you in a
Very special way
Kind of – still...
A part of the real
Human race by daily
Making decisions no
Matter if its good or
Bad its keeping you
Alert and produces
A plus each day daily
And in a good way
Just be careful
Of your safety each
Day in what you do
Think things thru and...
Continue to be a part
Of creation the creator
Made for you.

Future

Thru the back window fast approaching
To pass by with roving eye
One's future may then go by –
To be waiting , waiting,
With watchful eye, for one to touch-
Unknown.
Pass by , the future –
To become… the past.

A Feeling

Most each evening
There's a feeling that
Comes on
About 8:45 pm on
I usually haven't eaten
And don't usually from
That time on till
Much later do I then,
The task of eating venture
On.
It seems this feeling
Is very strong taking
Or very strongly taking
Anything else at the
Time that I'm busy with
Usually engaged with
Or upon and gives
This stupefied
Uncontrollable –
Seemingly feeling of
Lonesomeness to
Venture on where
Just emptiness and
Nothingness is all
About in the house
Or there about.
Where one can gaze
And have a feeling of
Almost nothingness
Or on the other
Side of the coin, really
Nobleness come about
But if I think of my
Wife or other family
Member of my home
That's left and gone
Especially of my wife

That's recently most
gone away any member
seems to come anytime
called upon or any day
right to my upper left
not to high and right
away with words of
consolation really
nice speaking naturally
soothing warmly just
like they were there
and not away.
After they've talked
This feeling calms
Down.
Most time in maybe
80 or 90% goes away,
This comes most
Evenings now when
I'm home now not
Away.
Sometimes other times
I'm not busy too
In the day.
But its getting better
And when it comes
Family members others
Help drive this feeling
Which I hope soon and
It now seems to be
Getting coming less
When bouts like this
Come along much
Often
My son and his wife
Calls invites me to
His home or goes out
To restaurants sometimes

continued

continued

Continues...A Feeling

Also this I consider
A very nice thing to do, they may
Be having the same problem,
Recently same as I
Tho he still has his
Wife close by which
Helps pull one thru
Like pleasant notes
Of lovely song.
Where only music
Comforts long.
These restaurant visits
Home folks family
Talks and all of what
Is now was before
And family togetherness
Now is strong and
Helps mend also is
Helping pull us all
As one together
And in its silent
Very silent way when
This feeling evenings
Anytime comes on
Comes rushing thru.

Deep Water

In life
When your boat
Gets in –
Deep water
And everybody's boat
Gets in deep water
Sometime
It don't matter
How much time
Or how you do
Or what you do
As long as its honest
And true
And it gets you thru
In life
When your boat
Gets in deep water
Get you, your boat
And your
Crew –
Thru.

Days

Yesterday I've tucked away-
Today, I'm still using today,
Tomorrow, day after tomorrow – maybe go fishing
Sounds good to do. Days , days they're most
The same- we give them names- we do
To help us do what we have to do , they give
Us the seasons, months, years, too- it's
Beautiful what the days can do.
Yesterday tho, I've tucked away-
Today, I'm still using today.

Gathered

After a lovely dinner and friends
Are gathered near- memories are discussed
That suddenly appear- it kind of seems,
A certainly, a certain- love is near.
After a lovely dinner
And friends, and memories,
Are gathered near.

Heavenly

Beautiful sky of
Crystal blue with
Moderately drifting
Clouds of white give
An unforgettable
Memorable view
A heavenly sight, from the sky.

A Beautiful Thing

On a hill where children and birds play,
Grass is green there too
Where clouds drift by
Giving open sky,
And the sky is crystal blue
And the children wave
As the birds wings
Flutter near the hilltop high
Oh… tis a beautiful thing
To the watchful eye-
The hilltop brings
With the children,
The birds,
And the open sky.

Each Day

The assurance of,
Morning
Noontime   too-
Rains when they're
Given
Brings nourishment
Too
And birds that fly
Bring joy to …
The sky
And beauty's free
As days pass by
Thru love that's
Free and care
That's given
As moon, stars
Clouds, sunshine
Too
Like the assurance of …
Morning from
Creation,
Each day- spiritually
Beautifully always
Lovely faithfully
Eternal-
And true, all way thru.

Thrown

Throw … This away
Throw that away-and, then …
Throw all that old stuff, have it
Just, thrown away- cause …
Old folks keep a lot of
Things,
The young folks think
They should
Throw away
And, we old folks- this,
Perhaps, tho- reluctantly …
Should, do.

Racing

With racing clouds
Across the sky
A change of weather
May soon be
Nigh.

Your Day

With sunshine
To brighten enlighten
Your day
A touch of blue sky
Along the way
A wish, a hope
And who can say
What one can accomplish
On such a day

Don't Look Back

Remember, remember
But don't look back
To look back you might
Stumble and fall
Wouldn't be good
At all
Don't need to fall
If you do tho get up
Dust yourself
Keep on thru
Remember, remember
Don't look back, keep on track
Keep on … thru.

Prepared

Ready is to be prepared
Be ready to do battle
The bad to settle
The good to be
Successfully
Settled
Ready is to be prepared
Nothing to be feared
All that is promised
Is given
So wonderful for all
To be
With creation prepared-
Ready, for whatever be.

Do

Morning pass's
Almost as before
For I'm near
Where folks are
And can talk with
See others as before
I take lunch with me
Sit in – use radio there to
And be in the car
So as to put off
So long, at home
Quiet alone
A little longer
When I get home
Then stay in garage
And do anything
First – before I
Open door to –
House quiet with me
Then – I clean,
Lunch box and be
With my pencil and me
And write and write
About almost –
Anything there be
And hours pass by
That is nice too
Its good its comforting too
For soon then –
When comes the night
I can feel – I can be
Oh yes, and I ride my bicycle
Too, that's really good to do
Then I read some too
But not much at night
Anymore.
I do write anytime
I catch an imagery

Continued

Of something to write
A poem or story of
That's fun to do and
A good way for me to
Express my feelings thru
And leave my thoughts
Of moments passing
Of what I think, see,
Feel for others to see
Thru and quiet me
Individually thru also...
Its healthy to do.
Part of what I feel
Now that life as
It changes comes
Daily to us with
Love for each its
Special way is about
Each given day.
And we use it
And express it to
Other and ourselves
In our own way daily.
And the birds – and the stars
And the sun – and the moon
And the twilight too
We folks and we watch them
Our way – their way
Passing silent thunderous thru.

Your Bed

Make your bed up every morning
It helps to make a better day
Make your bed up every morning
It helps spruce up your day
Make your bed up in the morning
It's a good way to help,
Start the day – a neat way.

Of Rest

A day of rest –
Is nice to see, and –
Come about and be.
It may come about
And always does each week
On a Sunday because...
That's a day that's –
Set aside as a day
Of rest by the creator
For all, both big and small
To rest from everything.
Other days as they come
and pass –
tire us
As they pass thru
a holiday comes
And they do
a day set
Aside for rest for all, by all.
From daily work to rest
from work
And to do this
Is restful – is beautiful
Refreshing the body, the mind
The families, in
Proper ways, with lovely
And the relaxing … of rest.

The Moon

To holler at the moon
To holler when
There's no moon
There's no moon all,
By yourself
In a room
Cycles in you
And in you – round
And round
In your head
And body round
Then out the mouth
With lonesome
Sound (a scream)
From inside round
Like... "   "
To holler – (howl)
Holler at the moon
And from you – inside, from –
Inside and out. Sometime happens.
Then all is with time, ok.

Take's

It take's time for water to soak in
The ground – after a good rain.
It take's time- for the mind to comprehend,
The whistle of- an approaching train
It take's time for the new to soak in too
For everything … there is a time.
Give with love – with ,
Good understanding … of, that time.

Looking

Two birds just came
To that big tree over there
And they're looking this way
To see-what they
Can see , over here-
From over there.
Two birds.

Our Way

Fifty nine years ago
Today
In a land far far away
Across the ocean
In Japan
Yokohama Japan
Today on
30 November 1951
In the Am, Consular office
There far far away
We were married
Haruko
Fifty nine years ago
Today
Tho you left
April 15, 2010
This year
You'll always be
With me
As of that day
Fifty nine
Years ago today
And with the love
We shared
With each other
And thru the years
Together
Our way.

A Way

Music, music has
A way with you
That just – reaches thru
And touches something
Deep – deep inside
That always, always
Seeks, hides away
From light of day
And then responds
To certain music
Sounds.
Especially when sadness
Happiness or holidays
Like Christmas, thanksgiving
Or times that's special
To someone is around
Or even a memory
One has tucked away
Deep, deep inside
Can be found.
Music certain kinds
To certain people
When its heard
Has an effect that
Has the ability to
Reach inside a person
Wake up a memory
Bring that memory
Bring that memory
To life – float one
Away to a fantasy
Land. Transport one
Away to another time
With another person
People, time, far far
Away or near
Whatever certain
Music one may hear
Believe me music is
Wonderful, music is beautiful
Music has a way is
Like sunshine – to a day

The Holidays

Its been since April
That you left
April 15th
I remember
You're not here
There's a something
Now the holidays
Are here
Its something
I can feel
Perhaps its only me
But its something
Like a something
Really close
That lives
Within
That's always there
That's near
That always will be
That cares
That feels
That watches
That helps
and to
That's as the sunrise
Sunset too
With you. Has a spot
Understands
As you
Will be a member- its you perhaps
Tho not here
As before- but memories stay
Its been since April
And all,
Not the same, now…
The holidays are here-with you too,
Near-that's nice

Christmas Tree

From an old piece of masonite
A little, teeny
Christmas Tree- I made for me
For Christmas
After you left
On April 15th 2010
And it served for me
My Christmas tree.
I kept it in- a cabinet too
And still do
My Christmas tree
My little teeny
Masonite Christmas Tree
And…
I'll always feel-you were
With me
That Christmas
Christmas 2010
And that you'll always be
With me.

Caw

Two birds were saying
Caw
From way over there
Maybe they were
Crows
Because , crows say
Caw
As they sit , or they fly,
And it might be their way to say
Caw, Caw, Hi
Those two birds-over there
Maybe…
Said Hi.

All – Do

The months
Are going by - just in
Like a storm passing
Seems –
That it does fly.
Making
A rainbow too
Come,
Seemingly
And shining thru
That's life – I think
Amid strife
As months go by
They slow
They fly
They're all the same
And pass the same
And will remain
We slip – we slide
And then we glide
And slide
And glide
And pass – with months
Then pass as
Night right thru
In fact,
All do.

Singing

Little red wagon
Rolling along
Children pulling it,
Singing
Happy songs

Power Of Love

The powers of love
Reach far
No matter where – ere
You are
If the power of love
Reach you
Love can reach thru
To you
Across oceans
Thru countries
Thru – out the world
And touch
Find
Reach you
And connect
As light – thru dark
If the power of love
Is to be
And...
If the power
Of love
Is true to be
It is forever
And will stay
And forever be
Like sunlight
Like moonlight
Like stars in the sky
As a path way
Reaching – binding
Joining love
Of love
Together – for
The powers of love
Reach far
No matter where – ere
You are
The power of love
True love
Can reach thru –
To you.

The Healing

Tomorrow is just
Another day
Now that's just
Hip hip and hooray
The holiday's are
All finished
All gone on their way
With tinsel, toys
Homemade joys
Nuts and such
N' all that stuff,
Now can be –
Regular things
With
Regular days and –
Just, come what
May.
That will fit me better
Cause...
This year found me
Not feeling –
Quite the same
As years gone by
For some one left
With love
That years build by
But left a love
That love builds by
And it will take
Just days and weeks
Thru time and
Friends thru thoughts
Like something
Found – in the quiet of
A forest – or the faithful tide
Or – the glimpse of dawn –
Twilight as day more along
All this with time
Mixed with honest
With honest
To myself and
Love I, in true

Continued

I feel
Now holidays have
Moved on their way
And thru
Regular days are
Here again
With regular ways –
Will help to
Mend and help
The healing
Gradually – slowly
In more
Regular days
Again
Letting lovely
Lovely
Something lost
Flow-quiet...
Building-filling
With honest
Feeling
Thru love,
Back in.

Fine

Seems like - when, eatin and sleepin and all
Are in line- why everything goes along just fine
But when eatin don't fit
Or sleepin don't fit
Cause one slips a bit, or the other slips a bit
Or sumpthin or the other-just don't fit
Why everything suffers,just a little bitty bit.
But when all get together and , all get in line
Why everything goes back to bein just fine.

Red Wagon

The little red wagon
Mostly stays
Where children play
And it stays right there,
All day. Where …
Children play.

Trains

Choo , choo trains-are hard to find
Trains don't go
Choo , choo anymore, anytime.
Now… trains blow horns, like-
Cars, and buses do
Trains just don't go- choo, choo, choo
Anymore today
Choo , choo trains are like
Dinosaurs, they have all, just… Gone away.
Choo ,choo trains,
Those choo, choo, trains.

Tonight

I know its been
A long time
Since you left
But not too long
Seems like only
Yesterday
I know tho – cause
I'll never forget – ever
It was... September 15, 2010
About 11 pm
But it seems like
You're here tonight
Every where
Kanna and Haruka
Said they are coming
Tonight supposed
To be here about
11:00 – or 11:30 pm
Maybe you're waiting too
I can tell I certainly can,
Feel you're near
Its a good feeling too
Its the same feeling
We've had together
For years and years
That's why – I'm sure
We're together, like when we-
Raised our family
Seen our grandchildren
Your relation
My relation and
Everything we had, those
Many many, happy years
Together, I'm happy
We could do that
I think our creator
Meant for us to
Do that and I and
I'm sure you too
Thank our creator

continued

The Country

For our beautiful
Years together
I certainly feel
You're here a lot
Of times – its a
Good feeling too
And I feel it tonight
Stay here – stay here
Always stay near
I want you near
Because...
Love is beautiful
And we had
Many, many years
Of together
Lovely years together
Love is beautiful
I know its been
A long time
Since you left
But not too long
Seems like
Only
Yesterday.

Oh the country – has a way
To hush noise and blare away
And let quiet and beauty
Have its way
For there on a little hill top - fair
With beauty
All around – where-
We could see, for miles
With hardly sound
And birds, sunshine,
Blue of sky near
We left a dear friend there
With other friends
Quite near
And with the creator
Our love – creations love
To be
Then we left
Went on our way
Together, to gather-
And mingle friendly
With friends
And that same day
With plans for meeting
With and thru love
On other days...
Oh the country has a way
Of keeping love
Of keeping life
Altogether, lovely
Quietly beautifully...
In, creations way
And we can visit – with our friends
In the country – that cemetery,
Anytime, most any day.

Lovely Ways

After some one you know
Been really really close
For many many years
Your spouse, your wife
Your close, I mean close
Best friend.
And you've been there near
Right there for 58 years
Till the very, very end
And you were there right
Close, right close, even then
Why it has an effect
That I think always
Stays not quite like
At first, but fades
Some but stays, for
Always thru close
Love in a way
For that close is strong
Built like an old old
Tree, from and thru
Years of belonging and
One builds it quiet and
For free and it lives
On on and on, it stays
I think till both are
Planted and then lives
On in the rest of
The family.
And is felt very
Much on the first holidays
After someone close
Real close has left –
Gone away, seems things
During once really

Continued

Continues...Lovely Ways

Happy, happy holidays just
Slide by with hardly any
Feelings almost like
Just blank days going by
Maybe if more days
Holidays pass by
And there's been more
Time for all to pass
Thru and the lovely
To really settle in
My thoughts will be differed
Some friends church friends
We now left, one during
The holiday one night
After.
That started the process
Almost from start again
Its kind of fading
With me.
But its still there
Guess it always will be
Feels good in a way
Like someone cares
Very much in
Lovely, lovely
Ways.

Always

AlwaysContinues...Always

Living together
For a long long time
A bond is formed
That flows with me
When one departs
The pace is changed
The bond that
Was formed
No more remains
That world – has been –
Dismantled
Practically, torn apart
And must be –
Reassembled
To continue as one
A world of one
Minus one
The world of one
From the world
Of two
Is similar – to walking
With shoes of four
With shoes of four
With feet of two
Quite hard at first
But with adaptation
And practice
One can do
For the world of one
Is a quiet also
Thunderous one
For much must be done
To keep the world
Of one
A functioning one
And a fairly
Happy one
All at the same time
Forming the bond

continued

Of one
To the world
Of one
While each day flows
Over
In silence in
Readily accepting
Each ones choice
To flow
With the days
On
For each day flows
As a river
Forever and on
Tho living together
Or living as one
The world accepts
Each day accepts
Flows on world on
With new – with old
Forming bonds
With each
In silent love
Individually
Permitting a bond
With the earth
That's permanent
For all
Forever –
And each ones world
With the earth
Thru creation
With creation
Flows
As an –
Eternal river
On
Forever and ever
On
Always.

One

One from two
Leaves only one
That grew –
From two
To one.

Now
One must do
What two
Did do.

No...
The world accepts
The world
Of one.

If –
The world
Of one
Accepts
The world
Of
All
And lives
As one
With all.

Seen

I seen a little Lizard
That just stopped
And looked at me
Then walked away
And no more
Of that little Lizard
Did I see,
All day.

Floating

Some seen her floating
Just o'er the water
In the night
All dressed in white
They said she was
Looking for -
Her children
She had some way
Lost before
And she herself
Had lost – her way
Some see her
When she comes
This way
Most by night
And seldom day
Looking searching
All her way,
The lady dressed –
And all – in white
Floating quite,
O'er the water...
In the night.

Told Me

My friend told me
That in a house
Sometime they hear
Dishes rattling
Knocks and
Kicking doors
And walls
Sometime –
And no ones there
Or anywhere
I wonder who –
Just who,
Is passing thru
My friends house.
And why - and what
Are they
Trying to do?

Guidance

Its been a little
Over since a year now
Since the wife left
Its lonesome in
The house
With no other sound
No other voice
Than my own around
I think of ghosts
And poltergeist
Their partners etc.
That we hear of
In movies radio shows
People speak of and
All, and kind of
Wish some would come
To break the silence
Just come on call
But the silence prevails
None come near
Least none I can hear
So I've got accustomed
To this way of life
Now think that's the way of life
Now I think that's the
Way somehow its to be
Still converse my way
Love still is the same
For my wife and always
Will be.
From when we met
Years ago in Japan 1948

Continued

Continues… Guidance

Till now that somehow
Started an eternal
Flame for us. That
Still burns bright
With a light of love
Like heaven light
With love eternal
That goes on forever
And keeps us in touch
In a way we understand
And always will
This will always be
Silent for just we
Two and joining from
A far as gazing at a
Star can do, and give
A silent love from
Far away as light to
Dark and dark to day
Tho its been a little
Over a year now
Each day brings new
And understanding and
Also with a light
That shines I feel with
You and creation that
Helps with guidance
As we move thru.

BYE

Of Lovely

Think of the blossom
The flowers too.
Think of a seed-
A sapling-a small-and...
Large tree too.
Think of an egg,
Small, medium-large bird too.
Think of a cloud, a storm-
A rainbow too.
Think of dawn, sunlight
Happiness, a beautiful day too.
Think of noon, twilight
Evening, moonlight, stars-
Just shining thru.
Think of all this...
With family, flowers
Sunshine, storms
Rainbows, twilight, evenings.
Aged with love-
And...
Of lovely memories,
Too.

Understand

Feeling lonesome
Wanting some one near
Lone some, lonesome
Fear- no fear
Hard to under stand too
Hard to see thru
But see thru too
Since you went away
Cloudy- some sunshine too
Know that's what you'd want
And the way you'd want it too
Cause that's the way we done things
All the way thru- but...
Feeling kinda lonesome
Hard to understand- but understand too
Hard to see thru- but see thru- but see thru too.

Lead you

Sing to yourself
When there's no one around
Sing to yourself
Let music lead you around
You'll be happy
You done this
In your own way
You'll be led from night
To light of day
When you feel that way
Sing to your self
When no ones around
Let music lead you around
From night
To your, light of day.

0f Flowers

Little children's fingers
Pick the flowers
Of springtime
Springtime days, springtime ways
And grow as flowers
Day by day
Children, flowers
Days and hours
Little fingers picking
Picking....
Springtime flowers.

Shadow

Little bird
With your shadow
On the ground
I know you're up there
Flying around where are you going
With your shadow
From up there
Where are you going
Way up there
Flying in the air … little bird ?

Children Dancing

Dancing dancing
Children dancing
Exercising too
Dancing dancing
Children dancing
Fun they're having too
Dancing dancing
Children dancing
Long they're dancing
When you
Dance, dance-
Children dancing
On and on and on
They're dancing … till,
They're dancing thru.

The Sky

I seen a crow
Flying in the sky today
And that crow up in
The big open sky
Can fly many places
Or
Right close by
While you and I
Watch that crow
In the sky.
I seen a crow
Flying in the sky today
Up, up that crow
Went
Then far, far away.

Dancing Too

Older folks
They're dancing
In their way they're dancing
Slower slower too
Dancing, dancing, dancing
Soon they,
Their dancing-danced,
Thru.

Preschoolers

The preschoolers are
Graduating today
Going to kindergarten too
Years pass fast
Soon they will be with
Education thru
Ready for
Well
Who knows
The preschoolers are
Graduating today … and-
The world is waiting,
The world's way.

A Nice Day

Blue sky
A few clouds
Windy too
A nice day
A Spring day
In Salinas
Is passing thru
Salinas, California
Today- with, blue …
Of sky.

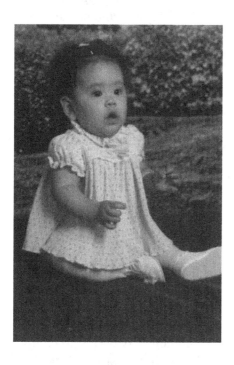

Shadow

The shadow of a crow
Just passed by
I seen the crow
Flying to, I know not where
Not too high, in the sky
The shadow of a crow
Just passed by.

Quite a Sight

Watching evening turn to night
Thru my patio window
Is quite a sight
And it's raining lightly too
Daylight is fading
Fast away dark is consuming
Light its way
Soon dark and rain
Will rule the night
I hear the rain just
Pattering down
Falling on the roof top
And the ground
Thru the dark just of
Tonight
While I watched thru
My patio window
Evening…
Turn to night and,
It's quite a sight.

Spring

Its February now
It's almost spring
The days are getting
Longer
A little more sunny
Too
Trees will blossom
When spring comes
Thru
And the blossoms
As they come
Then flower, together as -
They do, blossoms, flowers,
Nature's way, then -
Will show us
In a way
The power of
A love to us,
In the creators
Way
Imagine, why
It's February
It's almost Spring.

Have

Everything it seems
Moves some
When the wind blows
The trees move
The grass moves
The clouds move
Tree leaves move
Most everything it seems
moves some
when the wind
blows thru
yet…
I've never seen
The wind
Have you?

Children Danced

The children danced today
To their chosen song
Their chosen style
And way
The parents came and
Watched
While their children
Mostly 4 and 5 years old
Danced on stage today
I'm quite sure the children
The parents, the teachers
Will remember as special
Today …
The children danced,
Today.

Dragonflies Today

I seen dragonflies today
Not near the water
But quite far away
They were flying
Near a building
Flying this way that way
All over
Near that building today
I like to watch
Dragonflies when they fly,
Their way.
It's interesting
To watch dragonflies
Fly
I seen dragonflies
Flying today.

Kinda

Kinda late in the day
Kinda lazy, hazy too
And the mountains
Hills stand out
In an interesting way
Cause twilights coming soon,
To kinda- end the day
In a sort of
Lovely way
Right now, it's toward-
Evening - night
Also, it's getting kinda late
Kinda, late in the day.

The Hillsides

Oh the hillsides in Salinas
In July are golden brown
Standing tall
Out in the sunshine
That seems forever all around
In the spring they're
All green with grass
In July, brown far away
There's a beauty
In the hillsides tho
Hazy blue
At times of day
That just special
Seems its … just, for you.
As are Salinas skies,
Of blue.

Given

Blessings, blessings
Given by God
We mostly never understand
Will later perhaps
Much later
Then we understand
The necessity
Of the blessings needed given
Wonderful
When needed
Fully and
With love
Blessings, blessings
From above of
Forgiveness and love
Needed- given.

Clouds

The clouds were down
Close to the water
I could see a little hill
Not too far away
And rocks of
Small and big
Near the shore line
As I walked from the wreck
Thru deep of water
Toward shore
Seemed close
Seemed far away with
Clouds down
Near the water
And murky sunshine
Shined thru clouds
Of late evening sky
That day
Watching, me...As
I walked.

Summer Day

The sun is warm today
Not really, really hot
And with it's soft , soft breezy breeze
The day is warm
Tho hot it's not
It's just a warm with sun
Mid soft of breeze, a breezey way-
And a beautiful
Summer day.

Mistakes

Mistakes mistakes
Others look for
Others mistakes
Judging , judging
In their way
Others each and
Everyday
The creator only
This can do
And does it by
Our actions too
Mistakes, mistakes
This all do
Only the creator
Judges– really judge's,
Only the creator can truly this
Do.

Used to Be

When I went back
To see
The little town
Where I was born
Where I grew
As a child
Not much was changed
Seemed a lot
The same
Of course
The house,
The school, were gone
Old friends were gone
For twas nearly seventy of-
Years.
Years seem to fly
Just go sailing by
Things just don't wait
For you
As they go thru … and,
This I did - find
When I went back to see,
The little town where I used to be.

The Fruit

Camping was I
Alone I thought too-
Washed some fruit
Set it on the table to dry
A bird came along
Out of almost nowhere
To enjoy – with , I
The fruit…
While camping, was I.

Trust

Birds they trust too
In a day to day
Bird kind of way
Till to move
Most any kind of way, and-
People always do
Most all the time
Most any day
When you move
Birds
Don't seem to trust you
Any more.
And-
They fly away,
That's the way
Birds live
Everyday
And that's ok-
Birds
Live that way.

Firing

They're firing, they're firing
They're firing today
I can hear them firing
They're firing today
The firing range where
The law enforcement and others
Can fire their weapons
Is near where I'm camping
I can see them from far away
And hear them quite well
They're firing, they're firing
They're firing at targets
They're firing today.

Forget

I'm camping now today
I forgot to bring
My little pocket
Writing pad
I feel so lost without it
And surely wish
I had it
To write the many
Many natural things I see
In their natural settings
That I see
So very, very, plentifully
While camping
Gosh I really really miss
My little pocket
My small pocket
Writing pad
And wish I would
Have brought it
With me
But I didn't my
Oh my, oh my
I don't have it and I'm camping now today
But that's ok
I simply love, that I'm camping.

Rained

It just rained and rained
And then it stopped
To real hard rain
That It did not
It just rained and rained
And then it stopped

Beautiful Today

It rained some last night
The air is damp today
The sun is starting
To shine thru the clouds
I can see it in spots
On the hills far away
Mixed with blue on
The mountains
In the distance away
And it's quite beautiful
To view, beauty's way
It rained some last night
The air is damp today
It's autumn today,
It's an autumn day
It's beautiful, beautiful,
Very- beautiful today.

The Clouds

It's thundering, its thundering
The clouds are getting dark
Way over on one side
Of the sky
The other side has now
Lots of blue of sky
But it's thundering
Thundering louder too
I wonder, I wonder
Is a storm
A big storm
Coming today,
For its thundering
Thundering
And…
The clouds are getting
Dark,

It's– that kind of day.

Calling

The crows are calling
They're calling
They're getting together
They're flying together
Now they're turning away
Oh, maybe they're calling
Because they want to fly
That way, far away
And, that's what they're doing
Too.
They're flying away and
Calling, calling.

Storm

After the thunder
Lightening a little
Came too
Now its raining
It's rained for nearly
30 minutes
I think a little
Storm is passing
Thru
Maybe that's what
The thunder later lightening
Was preparing for
This storm that now is,
Passing thru.

Remember

The rain has finished
The suns coming
Out again
The clouds are down
Low
So low they are moving
Down next to
The mountains near
Where I'm camping
Passing down thru the valley
And it's so strange
They're usually so high in the sky
Now down low with me
Where I can close see them
Down in the valley
Of course one has
To remember
Rain, sunshine, clouds
Too are all
From the creator
And the creator
All can do.

A Dragonfly

I see a dragonfly
Dead on the floor
I wonder what happened
To that dragonfly
I understand
A dragonfly
Is first a water beetle
Then a dragonfly
To fly gracefully
As a dragonfly
Then to die on the floor
Never more to fly
That's the first time
I ever seen a
Dead dragonfly
I wonder what happened,
To that dragonfly-

That dragonfly, I see.

An Airplane

I hear an airplane
Flying by
In the night in the sky
Over the clouds
In the dark flying by
I just heard an airplane
Flying by in its space
In the dark,
In the sky.

Writing

I've been writing, writing
Writing where I'm camping
Out today
I've been writing, writing
Writing almost all day
I've been writing on a story
That I'm thinking
On,
To write about-
I've been writing, writing
Writing where I'm camping
Today, while I'm camping
Camping out.

Night-Dark

Night and dark
They live together
As one
Night and light
In dark
They live as night
With light
In dark
Night with no light
And dark
They live together
Again
As one just…
Night and dark.

Tires

Tires, tires, we use tires
On lots of things we have, and do
On , buses, cars, trucks, airplanes, bicycles
Toys, other things- too.
Tires, tires ,we must have tires
To do the things we do.

After the Rain

After the rain
I can see thru the clouds
And it's near dark
I can faint see
The mountain tops
I can see clouds
White clouds drifting
Slow on the mountain sides
I can see house
Lights on too
And a car lights
Descending
On a hillside
I can see night
In the damp dark
Coming on after
after the rain.

After

It's after the rain
I see the butterflies
I didn't see them during
The rain tho
But I see them now
In the sunshine
That's trying to peek
Thru the clouds out.
The butterflies are
Tho small
In size
So quietly
Quietly fly,
The butterflies, beautiful
Viewing their world
As they move- most silently,
Thru the world
After rains or, most anything-
Where they fly- has passed.

What's

What's usually expected
Hardly ever comes
And the unexpected
Does
It's supposed to rain
And it doesn't
The planes always late
And it isn't
Not this time
It's early, very early
And you almost miss it
Then its supposed to snow
For Christmas
And it does, proving
What's usually expected
Hardly ever does
And the unexpected
Does
How about that.

Lights

Lights in the dark
Where they stay
Have a place in the dark
Far away
Maybe they belong to a house
Maybe they belong to a
Light post
Maybe they belong to
A person
Or maybe they came
From a planet far away
Reflecting that light to you
In someway
If that's possible
Is   it ?
But lights in the dark
Where they stay
Have a place in the dark
Far   away.

As I Gaze

As I gaze out the window
Of my van where I'm
Camping
There's only one other vehicle
Down the campground
From me
It's real quiet out here
I think, let's see- maybe
Those lights in the valley below,
In the little town down there
Otherwise it's quiet in the dark
Early in the morning too
But that's ok I wanted this way
And it's been that way too
Because I want it quiet too
Because I want it quiet so,
I can write
It's really, really quiet
There's supposed to be mountain lions
Out here too so far I've seen.
Two deer and a little lizard
And it's quiet and nice as
As I gaze out the window of my van
Where I'm camping.

Fast

A Noise in the quiet
Gets your attention
Fast
Because it makes you
Think quick
Very quick
When there's no other...

Noise.

Noise

Where is that noise ?
What makes that noise ?
That noise that
Meddlesome noise,
That's disturbing my quiet
My precious quiet
That's mine, mine
While this quiet-
Lasts
What, just what's
Making that noise?

Watched

I watched the cars
Go whizzing by
And where they go
I know not
And I also know
They did not know
That I right here
Watched them go by
Go whizzing, whizzing, whizzing by.

Those whizzing cars.

Of Way

It's a nice day today
In a cool cloudy
Kind of way
Suns shining gray
Thru the clouds
Mountain's with blue
Haze roundabout
Maybe from the clouds
Hanging low
Maybe in the afternoon
The sun will come out
If it don't, it will still
Be a nice day
In a cool, cloudy
Kind of way.

Views

People have different view's
Of everything they see
What I see and my view
For me is maybe
Not the view you see
And what you see
From your view
Is not the view
For me
People have different view's.
Of everything they see.

Finished

Camping trips all finished
Going home today
Had a good time
Done some reading
Quite a lot of writing
Had a good time passing hours away
Camping trips all finished
Going home today

A Little Bird

I see a little bird
Hopping on the ground
Down among the bushes
Hopping all around
I see you little bird
I'm watching you
Little bird
I'm watching you, I'm watching you
While you are hopping
On the ground, hopping all around-
I see a little bird.

Shoreline

There's a spot on the ocean shoreline
Where the stones are large and small
And the water of the ocean
Stands quiet, low at times
Near these stones of large and small
Then at times the ocean water
Roars at times as thunder where
These stones do lie there too
And the clouds sometime
Most touch the water there
At times this, there they do
Then at nights with clouds
The moon peeps down with
Mystery there too and by day
The sun it watches this shore of
The ocean too
Few know of this shore but I do
I seen it in a picture someone painted
That I bought, others maybe
Seen it too- this spot on the,
Ocean shoreline of those stones, both large and
small.

A Nice Day

Its bedtime now the day is thru
Been a nice day too
Went to a restaurant not too far away
Had a nice meal
Visited there
Passed time away
Visited too
Now this days hours have
Slipped away, its bedtime
This day is thru
Been a nice day- too.

Campgrounds

One of my favorite campgrounds
Where I like to go
Pass many an interesting happy
Hour away is in
The state of California
At laguna Seca … County of Monterey
Site sixty and seven
There to me the scenery's just right
It overlooks a valley
With a little village below
And mountains around
Where clouds pass thru
And distant mountains are
Blue distant, bluish blue
Hawks fly by chasing prey
From sky a crystal clear sky
Of which they, mostly are.
Also nights with stars there when
The all, is most beautiful
Quiet and quietly, beautiful
And I always go on quiet days
When there's
Little or no traffic too, at the
Busy, busy Laguna Seca Raceways
Its then I go to site
Sixty and seven
Over the valley there
And write and write
My poems and stories
Passing many an interesting
Hour away
At one of my favorite campgrounds
Laguna Seca in California …
In the county… of, Monterey.

In the Night

A shadow on the curtain
On the curtain moving
In the light of the street
In the night
You look slightly worried
Wonder
Find it's of the tree branches
Moving with
The wind in the night
In the streetlight
Moving branches
In the night
No need for concern
All is all right.

Nice Day

It's a little cloudy today
A little blue in the sky
Too
Not too cold not too warm
Just a nice day
With
A little cloudy today
A little blue in the sky
Too.

There Was

Across forever and always
In between there's
Never
It seems to be in-
That somewhere
That ever more
Strays to see
There if you stay
And then out
Into a mystery
Of nether almost,
Like light moon glow
And next to mixed
Starlight of dawn- then slipped
That way to you,
Across forever thru dark
And a lovely
Light you see-
The light of day,
Day light
Across forever and always.
It's there to see– twas,
There was … And-
May, be.

Watched

My cat she watched
Me trim the trees in my yard
Twas almost dark
Yet she watched me
Watched till I was thru
Seemed very interested too
I wondered if she wondered
Just what I was doing
To the trees she sharpened
Her claws and sometime
Climbed on, slept under
Too
My cat she watched
Me trim the trees
In my yard
Twas almost dark
Yet she watched close,
Till I was thru.

Handful

Grab a handful
Of dark
Take it in the sun
With you
But throw it away
When
You're thru
Cause
Dark won't stay
Long
In the sun
With you.

Ending

The noontime came along
Like notes of a song- with sunlight too
On it's way, then noontime moved to-
Twilight, evening- tucked daylight away
With night – moonlight , starlight- to light
The night, ending a most lovely day – smooth,
Like notes … of a beautiful song-
Things – moved along.

Abandoned

An old abandoned house
I seen
Along the railroad tracks
With a smoke stack
A long gone window
Black, against
The walls in back
A house of past
Yet…
With memories filled,
I just seen
Dreams with my roving eyes maybe
Someone's dreams while I
On the train
Sped by viewing
That old abandoned house
I seen of course, whose dreams-
That for sure,
I'll never know
Others do- tho.

Character

Like good soup
Is   Character
The very best
When put to test
Is homemade- and prized
As good soup,
Beautiful …
Jade.

Character– Character is.

Summer

Summer's   here
Summer's   here
Springs finished
Summer's   here
The grass is green
The hills are too
The sky is blue
Where birds can fly
And almost seem
To touch the sky
Summer's   here
Summer's   here
I just love summer
And   summer's here.

The Night

Lights of the night
From some fireflies
At night
Little lights on ocean waves
That glow of many
From just what
Of the night or why
I don't know
Will the wise inform me
Why those lights of the night
Glow, others too
All of their own sometime
A lonesome glow
When it happens too
In the quiet of the night
And causes
Lights of the night seen at times
By yourself
When that time of night is nigh
Is comforting though from the
Strange lights
Of the night that glow.

Spectacular

Owls of white
In the night- make a haunting
Spectacular sight
As you view
They view
Both view- each of you
By campfire light
In the night.
Owls of white
In the night
A very unforgettable,
Spectacular-
Sight.

Flying

Little airplane
I see you
Way up high
In the sky
Of blue – flying by
Where are you going
Oh so high ?
Cause I see you
Going by
In a blue, blue sky
Singing,
Singing your song
Flying   by,

Little– airplane.

Soaring

The birds they're
In the air soaring
Real quiet today
Not making much
Sound on this
Thanksgiving Day
Maybe they're thankful too
To be here and
Watch people
Happy and thankful
Together with
Others
Like they the birds
Are daily
While they soar
In air
Thankful
Like folks they
See today happy
On this
Thanksgiving Day,
Today are.

Rain

Tonight,
It rained a little
Not much at all
And when the rain
Began to fall
The night seemed
To change a little
Tho not much at all
Tonight, when -
The rain began
To fall.

That Kind

continues ...That Kind

I can remember
The house where I was born
The little town in Michigan
Where I was born
The people there were few
And houses there were few
Only one school house did stay
Close real close to my house
It did stay
One little church
And two stores
One pickle station
Also a railroad track
Where steam trains ran
Blowing whistles- ringing bells
Passing thru, and going back
Some folks there had cattle too
That roamed the town
Ate gardens too
Broke fences down
And the cows
They most wore bell's
That ringed as they moved
So all could tell
The animal was near
By the ting a ling, a linging
From the bell, as the cow
Ate grass, watching you
As you walked past.
Yes, I can remember
The little town where
I was born
The little town in the country
With gravel and dirt
Roads- the old steam train
Passing by,
The little one room school the,

Continues...

School's bell of my school
Ringing when the teacher
Pulled the rope.
And the open sky and
Season's changes
As I grew there- with friends
And family while the years
Passed rapid by.
I can remember
I can remember
And to remember
Is like a small vacation
From wherever- you may be
At that time, to a place
You can almost feel and see
The place you remember
For only you ...
It's that kind.

Has Come

Spring has come- the wondrous
Season of spring, winters gone
Spring is here- soon summer
Will come
Oh My ...
Has sprung,
The season of Spring
Spring has come, the wondrous
Season, of Spring.

To Stay

To have someone- for many years
Others grown- gone away
This someone goes away,
And back to earth to stay.
Then by yourself, only-
You then be
And by yourself, you stay,
Indefinitely.
The ways in which you
Then live, as one and only one,
Become much changed
For no one in the home
Each day is there, only you
You then- become
In a way
As two- to you
Invisibly-
And in your way, to you
Very slightly- carefully, too
When …
To have someone for many years,
Others grown- others gone
And, this someone goes away
And … back to Earth
To stay.

Times

Confused at times
But that's ok
It serves
To make a better day
In many kinds
Of different varied
Before unknown
Now different
New learned ways-
At times, confused.

Their Way

Dogs and cats to us
Are friends, very friendly
Dogs take us on walks
They seem to almost
Talk at times
Their way.
And cats too almost do,
Tho cats may
Turn their heads
Walk away, some days
And be more the animal
They be.
Dogs and cats
Remain, very friendly
They seem to almost
Talk at times
Their way.

Walking

Turn the page
Keep walking on
Thru the days-and
Thru the nights
Thru the mornings
Noon ,twilight
Thru books read
Then re-read too
Memorized-
In forehead ,back,
Right thru
One must …
Turn the page
Keep walking on
Always, always
Keep walking
Walking
On.

Miserable

Out in the rain
At night- in November
It is, just as-
Wet and cold And miserable
As it can be.
And if you are
Out there in it
You are too - just…
As wet and cold
And miserable as
You can be.
For its nighttime in
November and its
Raining too- that's
The way its supposed
To be.
Till the rain is thru.
Wet cold and real-
Real miserable, too
Miserable as it- can be.

Interruptions

Slight interruptions
During the day
May slightly hinder
In a way
May also shine
With sun , then light
Another's pathway
Placing us where we
Were to be
This slight interruption
During the day
Helping we, also others travel
Creations pathways,
During the day.

Climbing

I'm climbing
A mountain
Halfway to the top
Sometime-
Want to go back
Tho I'll never stop
Till I get to the top
And over it too
Then with the mountain
I'll be thru
I'm climbing this mountain
Perhaps…
Other mountains- too
Climbing, climbing
I'll never get thru.

The Ground

Fix the grpund
Prepare the grpund
Then plant the
Seed
In the ground
Watch the seeds
Grow all around.
But first
Fix the ground
Prepare the ground.

As Days Meander

Thanksgiving, Thanksgiving
A Thanksgiving Day
Just a beautiful
Calmly lovely of
Weather
Thanksgiving Day
Where you can
Walk, talk
With the children
Outside, inside
Too
Dine with
Converse with
Have just spend
A wonderful
Time with
Is a Thanksgiving
Thanksgiving
A Thanksgiving Day
To remember and
And cherish
For many days
As days meander,
Passing, thru.

To Pictures

Talk to pictures- talk to pictures
And …
They look at you- they stare at you
But answer you- they never do
When you- talk to pictures,
Talk to pictures, if … sometime,
That- you do.

Harmony

The world so beautiful
For all to see, and was created
In lovely harmony
Of – soil of brown, a Sun of yellow,
Snow covered mountains
A velvet black the sky of night
And flowers colorful beautiful
Like the rainbow
Also people created to fill the Earth
Are of similar colors, they seem to be
Of brown, black, yellow, white
Our world of Creation
So beautiful to see- was created
In lovely, lovely,
Harmony.

Different

The love of two, expressed
Over years of many, not few
Is quite much as viewing
Thru a mirror- which gives
A forward, rear too view.
If the mirror becomes clouded
Or one of the love
Is no more
Is, called away
Love of the two expressed
Thru the years- is still there
As viewing thru- a clouded mirror
Tho expressed …
In a much different,
Individual- way.

Pecking

The birds are on my house,
On the roof, today
I hear them pecking softly on the tile
They stay there for awhile
And then they fly away
They like the roof, for it is high
And gets them closer to the sky
So they can see
Far … far away
The birds are on my house,
On the roof, today.

Travelers

The birds they fly
So free- so high
The birds-
Are travelers,
Of the sky.

Of the sky, they fly.

The Blue

The beautiful blue- of the sky today
So beautiful blue
And so far away
I can see thru the blue
Way … high and away
Oh, the beautiful blue-
Of the sky today.

They Watch- They See

The birds they watch
From the chimney tops
The birds they watch the sun
As it drops, I see them watch
From the chimney tops
They watch from East, West,
North, and South
All sides of the chimneys
They watch, they watch
The birds they know
When evening's on it's way
And when the sun drops low
Till it has dim of glow
And night's on it's way
The birds they watch
And they fly away
To return as morning, returns.

Most days.

Brings Dawn

And they watch as dawn
Brings morning
Near chimney's
Other places- and
Many roof tops
The birds- they watch
The birds- they see
Most everything
Also,
You and me

They...watch.

Softly

Evening so quiet, floated in
Bringing dim of glow- to the sky
And night soft, softly came
With starlight, moonlight
To faint, fading glow of sunlight
In deep- open lovely of sky
The day-
Had gone
Away,
Softly … and by.

Padded

Cats walk on padded feet
They are so quiet
When they walk
You can almost hear
Ants when they talk or sing.
And what enormous thunder
That would bring
Just hearing ants
Talk and sing- while cats walk by,
On feet as quiet
As butterflies when they fly.
Cats are, oh so quiet-
Just quietly, quiet
When they walk.
Because …
They walk, on padded-
Feet- those cats...
They, do.

The Cat

On the car
The cat sit
Shadow on the wall
On the car
The cat sit
Not on the wall
At all.
Oh ...

Watch

Sit right here and watch
The night attract the day
And keep the day
Till night slips slow-
Away.

Nervously

Laughing, laughing
Nervously
But not really,
Really, in reality
Perhaps twas what
They seen and had came thru
Others had not seen,
And never would
At that time know-just why,
These few were
Laughing, laughing-
Nervously, and so.

Dead End

Dead end streets
Have bridges to the far, far away
Bridges difficult to see
Some can see- others cannot
And pass them by
Those bridges hard to see
To far, far away
Where most lucrative
Of treasures stay.
Those dead end streets
Those bridges, there-
Those ghostly bridges,
They …
Have much.

Noises

Noises, noises
Some we understand
Noises, noises
Some we understand not
Terrible, terrible
Haunting cries
That trouble some
Most of their lives
Like
In roars of the waves
To many of the brave
These noises, noises exist,
Some understood,
Some are not
To see they, cannot be-
But to feel, to some,
They be.

In The Morning

Early in the morning
When its quiet all about- and there's no one near
Just where you are , those times sometime
You think about the many places where you've
Traveled and folk's you've seen
And what it's meant to you
How you've enjoyed the many times and friends
You've made from things you've seen and plan to do
And then you write and write the more all thru the day
And most the night as things come to mind to you.
Cause…
That's what you came to this place for anyway, and-
It's what, that you must do especially when,
It's early in the morning and it's quiet all about.

Must be

A battle , a battle , a battle must be
To have a victory, and when a victory is won
Life's trouble it has again begun.
Tho to have a victory-
A battle, a battle must be.

Why

The utmost terrible that happens at times
Happens – for all to one and many
For reasons small or not any .
Of understanding at all tho-and is hard
To understand.
But happen it does the Creator understands
And comforts then waits to be
Asked why…
For before – and after
Of forgiveness- of the terrible that
Was done.

Remains

Like sunshine lights Heaven above
Let Christmas joy fill inside
With Eternal love and Christmas joy
With cheer that thru faith remains for years and years
Just lovely filled with love, making
A Merry Christmas Day
And a Happy New Year – that for
Years and Years is every year,
New… years , years thru.
Like sunshine lights Heaven above.

Passing Thru

Christmas time , with Christmas passing thru
No snow on the ground
No snow here green of grass all around
Christmas songs decorations too
Churches celebrating, people shopping
Christmas shopping trees, folks with Christmas deco-
rate.
Christmas time it's that time-
Christmas passing thru
Soon a New Year –New Year too
But now… it's- Christmas time, Christmas time
With – Christmas…
Passing thru.

So or So

Feelings , feelings come and go
Make each day just so or so
Feelings, feelings all can see.
Others see us this we know
Feelings, feelings tho… our feelings are of we
That shine like heavenly stars
Of where we are- what we do
Feelings, feelings come and go
Making our each and every day
Just…so or so.

The Christmas.

Christmas time with snow all around
Christmas time with grass all around
Christmas time with decorations too
Christmas time with Christmas music too
Christmas tme with children, family too
Christmas time with Military folks on
Battle fields, folks on street corners too
Christmas anywhere Happy there to be
Because if Christmas is in the heart
In love there deep and from the start melting snow
and
Ice away, leaving warm love to beam bright
About is for a Christmas with love .
That comes to all anywhere they be
For it's deep in the heart – and, that's the Christmas
to feel and see...When it's-
Christmas time.

Joyful

People somewhere filled with fear
People some places traveling there and here
People happy people sad
This most any time can be
Only now soon will be Christmas Day
A joyful happy time in an Eternal way
If felt as such deep in peoples hearts
Somewhere – someplace, anyplace
Thru faith,
That soon it will be
Christmas Day– an Eternal way.
For, most every where.

Years

After having lost a spouse of fifty years and more
Gives a feeling of loneliness
And deep respect
That is lovely in a way
And yet fulfilling too with a love that is near
And far away, and always there too.
Also a love
Of fifty and eight years
Beautifully given wonderfully too
Memories , memories
Remind of past, remind – of respect
Remind, with Respect.
After having lost a spouse
Of fifty years and more.

To Understand

When help is needed
To understand
What's not understood
In any way – night or day
With faith , ask the Creator
Night or day.
Get help
Faithfully- Eternally in
Ways beautiful, always-
When help is needed.

How

How will you know till you get there
How it's gonna feel till you get there
You can talk you can imaginary feel
But you'll never ever really know
Till you get there, how it's really gonna feel...Like,
When you get old, till you get there.
Then you'll know, and it's not so bad.
But that's the only real way to understand.
How you will know for sure
If Creation's good to you someday you'll know
And understand, the how- that's how.
When you get there.

Stride

Pride – to step back from your pride
Is hard to do, pride is tops
It keeps you at top in all you do.
Tho sometime you can just lower the pride some
and
See how you'll glide to tops, with galloping stride.

Duty

When the duty is the kind
That keeps one- wondering what's next, what's next
Then the duty is the kind
That maybe could go right or wrong
Or might end up as but… or as nothing
It could be this or that or maybe
We don't know what
Ones duty might then be best, to elsewhere be.
For one to have, even- duty.
When duty is the kind…that kind.

Train

I hear the whistle , can't you too
The train's a comin for someone too
Conductor's gotten his stepstool down
Train's a comin for someone
Train's a comin to town
The railroad's long gone – years ago
That's ok whistle's blowin
For someone , hear it blow
Don't need a ticket, or any rails
Get on board , you ain't a comin back
Cause you just be a ridin- ridin
Ridin somewhere,
Ridin, on those, magic … rails.
I hear the whistle, can't you too ?

Changing

Water beetles changing bodies-secretly,
From beetles…
To dragonflies
And changing – flying
Then with their friends
Off-
Into spacious
Skies.
As… dragonflies.

Find

Look for clouds – you'll find them
Look for sunshine you'll find it too
Look for storms- there's a way
Look , look for the way
You'll find it thru
May be difficult – look, look hard
The good will guide you thru
Look for clouds – you'll find them
Look for sunshine – you'll find it too.

Controlled

Grief and anger almost are one
They touch, but move aside just some
To let the level of the two
Sort of boil over but not put out the fire
That caused them both to well up so
With cause to be .
For they both inside controlled low real low below
Remain as winter- cold like snow
But breathing breaths…breaths of spring.
That-
Grief and anger – almost one do
As they touch , but move aside
Just some. They still are tho,
Almost same, almost one.

Unfold

Each evening is- the sum of dawn,
Morning, noon, afternoon, twilight, later,
Then … right before evening-dark or twilight
With long shadows of evening
Till night and dark thru dark-to dawn
And the same on and on
Each day to day as days unfold
Per evening, that is the plan…
Over and over , and over again
Again, and- again.
Has been, been for centuries
That plan… and-
Perhaps – twill be, twill be,
Twill always, be.
For sure, Eternally.

Planet

Mars , Mars so far, so near
So far, very far away
A planet we see every day
And wonder what do we see
That we see in sees way .
When we do- really see, on Mars everywhere
What …
Will we see ?
On Mars so far- so near
So far-very far, away, over-there.

The Valley

On the edge of the valley, where I'm camping
There's a village – I can see down below
And it's dark
And the light's – of the village
Look like little candles, in the dark-
They just glow, I can see them, where I'm camping
From the edge of the valley, down below.

Friends

Dark and lights of most any color and night
They're friends I think
Most times at nght
Wherever you see one
You see the other
Myself…
I think they're friends dark and lights, and night.
How about you-
What do you think ,
Do you think they're friends ?

Ourselves

In the quiet one can hear things
Like the ticking of a clock
Or how the wind blows
When tree leaves rustle
Their sounds are there most all the time
Tho it seems most other times
That at them to listen we're too busy-
Or we've forgot
But in the quiet one can hear things
And ourselves-
Almost , that- what , we think too… as we-pass thru

Since

Since I lost my spouse of many years
I go camping a lot
At a nice campground out in the country
Where I write in the quiet of
Days and nights
About what I see that inspires
Myself and yes, me
At the campground
Out in the country
Since I lost my spouse
Of many years.

August

A sunny day –a breeze here
Just a breath away
A bee over there
A bird soaring quiet by
No clouds – in the sky
Have to say, now…
That just describes a beautiful
Sunny with soft of breeze,
Lovely... An … August day.

The Mountains

I love to watch the mountains
Tho they never ever move
They're far away – far ,far, away
And ..
Just how they seem to touch the sky
But they never ever do, because…
The sky is high way, way high too
I love to watch the mountains
They fascinate me-
They really, really do.

Of Summer

So Spiritual-
So soft, the petals of the flowers of summer,
As they drift, with the month of August
Having came from far away.
Transplanted as the clouds that drift afar
Yet with beauty
Like the evening star
Shed light,
Heavenly light
Memories
Bright
And the flowers have a way
As they fade
As does the day,
To … leaves a fragrance,
As with love
Of their love-
From a flower of, soft-
The flowers …
Of summer.

The Butterfly

The butterfly rules with
Colors
The sky and quiet
As they fly
And when butterflies fly
There's
A beautiful lovely
Colors quiet,
Of so quiet
Beautifully- beautiful
Passing by
While butterflies
Of many colors
Fill their spaces
In the sky.

Seen

Last night
Seen a little snake on the camping ground
Restroom floor
Stuck it's tongue out at me too
Guess it didn't like me
Didn't see it this morning tho
It must have crawled out thru
The restroom door.
At least …
I hope so

Way

To sit the day till night away
And then till dawn
Till break of day
And then get up , move slow along.
One can spend time in that way
But it is not – in ,
The best of way.
To spend a day.
Tho some do.

I Hear

I hear a crow- I hear a crow
Don't see tho- don't see it tho
Can you tell it's a crow
If you hear it - don't see it tho
I can most times , I can
Tell it's a crow – when I hear a crow
I can most times I can
I hear a crow – I hear a crow
Don't see it tho- don't see it tho

Haze

Why do the mountains – of the faraway
Seem to get a bluish of haze
In the afternoon of the day.
And the rest of the hills
That are more close to me
Are of green that I do see
Why I wonder why do the mountains
Of the faraway
Seem to get a bluish of haze.
Tho they're beautiful when they do
In the afternoon of the day-
Get that way
I just wonder why

Flying Low

The hawks are flying low today
The hawks are flying low today
Little animals
Be careful on the ground today
The hawks are looking for you-
Flying low today
The hawks, are flying low today.
Looking – looking
Looking for you.

Range

There's a firing range near
My campground here
It's for police and others to use
So they can more accurate be
When they use their weapons to protect others
And you,
And yes-me

Milky Way

Dusting over many stars on high
Almost like a highway in the sky
Goes the milky way , with it's lovely light
Heaven high-
As seen from Earth
By you, and I.

Little Lights

Early in the morning- when dark seems all around
Everywhere close all around- just…
In it's way,
In a town near – but far away.
Their little lights in the dark
Look like they're placed there for you- to view
And bright those little lights seem to be.
When it's early in the morning , mid dark of night.
They're there to see– those lights,
While camping – from …
Where I be.

Christmas

Next week on this day
It will be Christmas Day – Christmas Day
On this day it will be
Christmas Day-
One week away
Some happy - some sad
Little children usually glad.
On …
Merry Christmas
Merry Christmas
Merry Christmas Day .And…
Next week on this day
It will be-
Merry Christmas Day.

A Trail

There's a trail I see – that winds up
The mountain to the top
Where it appears to stop
Maybe to let – the world pass by
While it views – and has
The wide open view of lovely
Heavenly spacious sky.
There's a trail I see
Maybe its watching the sky.

A Song

Singing a song if from the soul
And the whole of the song
From the soul it be
If the building where the song, is sung
If large it be – or if it be small
In the country, city, ship, mountain too
As the sounds reach out
Toward Heaven's high
If sounds out come thru
True from within – and the soul spills out
Maybe Angels hear, Maybe the Creator too
Songs from the soul, songs from the soul
Singing a song from the soul
For all to feel- feeling see as they meander out…
are,
Like flowers of spring
Like stars, clouds, nights, all can see Eternally.

A Few

A few purplish clouds
Way over in the corner of the sky
That I see are slowly moving
From where they be
To places I cannot see
So the blue of the sky
Can completely cover the sky
And make a beautiful day
It's own very personal way
These few purplish clouds today
I think , are being very , nice- today.

Grasshopper

One grasshopper
Was all I seen, while camping,
One grasshopper today
One grasshopper
Was all I seen
And then –
It jumped away.

Adrift

The clouds, the clouds I see white clouds
Adrift and in the sky
If the clouds were great hills of snow
Snow of white- white hills of snow
Drifting graciously slow
But high in the wide open sky
They would be hills of snow
Adrift in the sky
The clouds, the clouds
I see white clouds adrift…
And in the sky.

Always

When you've done something wrong
And you don't want others to know
Someones always watching you
You are…
Your mirror always tells you so
Just look at you
You so and so
When ever you've done something wrong
You don't want others to know
Your mirror always tells you
Quietly, usually lets you know
Just look-
Look in the mirror , at you.

Must Be

Recess - recess must be
In all things we may do
For rest , small rests
In all we do at times…
Well chosen times…
Enables better
Access to past and future
Things that…
We must do.
Recess – recess must be.

Understood

Be yourself – be yourself
Do your best , be good
Listen-listen too
And , you'll get thru
Slow on the way
Be understood – understand
Then faster too
Be yourself – be yourself
Do your best , be good
Listen – listen – listen too
And , you'll get thru.

Like This

At times like this – at time like this
We learned how to
Do what that we now do
There must be – times like this
For in times like this
From times like this
We learn how to
Do all that we
Must do.

Visit

Short visits good to do
Long visits overdo
Visit , visit
Good to do
Just don't ,
Overdo-
Visits.

Their Way

Snow is very beautiful
Dark much the same
They cover blemishes, on the ground
And all around
For night and day , not to be seen
Till they go away
Snow is very beautiful
Dark much the same
Shadows too
They have a way – their way…
When they pass thru.
They, very beautiful cover.

New Year

Christmas came this past Tuesday
New years now, on it's way
New year soon with sun and stars
Maybe a full new moon
New Year comes too
On next Tuesday…
New Year - Near Year's day
Coming too , a brand new year
A New Year's passing thru
Moving on it's way.

Beautiful Too

It's beautiful and not so sometime – but
Beautiful too
The days , the years
Given to us – each of us
As they - we pass by
On this place , the Earth.
And be , and see , and feel
Arrive on like, live
Return to
This Earth
It's beautiful
And not so sometime –
But,
Beautiful too
It is , it really is.

Writing

There's graffiti on the wall
Left for others
Like me to see.
There's graffiti on the wall –left
By others-for me to see of,
Their writings , that's ok but
Should be and could be better displayed in a
Book or other place.
Their knowledge of
Writing, drawing, is just lovely beautiful to see
But they put it in the wrong places and, in graffiti.

The Road

Don't do it now
Maybe you can do it later
Kick the can down the road- then…
It won't be such a load.
Nice to do it now tho.
But , not many seen it, the mistake-
They'll soon forget it
Don't do it now– tho...
Do it later- don't worry about it.
Just … Kick the can down the road.

Today

Just filled with
Today's and tomorrow's too
Day's pass quite loaded thru
I'll keep today as today
And make tomorrow
Today tomorrow
That way tomorrow
Won't fill up today
That's a better way.
Keep one day, as one day.
Filled– tomorrow today.

Anything

When you don't feel like doing anything
Do something good anyway.
Because everybody feels like not doing
Anything sometime at times
Hey… don't stop everything
Just do something good to do – that
Don't hurt anybody anyway.
When you don't feel like doing anything
Do something anyway
It will help you – in it's way
That's the way.

Paddle

Chase em- chase em
Paddle , paddle your boat as fast as you can
Straight ahead
There's the purse, see it-see it
Get there first, in this race
But look out
Careful- careful
You're going the wrong way
For today your boat
Has a hole in it
You'll get to the bottom first that way
Fix that hole someway
Chase em- chase em tho
Paddle as fast as you can
Follow the other's
That's the way.

Times

Perilous times- perilous times
Unrest all over the world
The kind of times – that tests
The swirl of all mankind to where folks don't know
Which way to go
To find a way – to get together as a union-
To relieve accumulation ot wealth
For health of all.
The base, the base, it seems is how just how
In a kind , kind way
To spread what is to all when some accumulate
The more of most of all
How just how to spread the rest in an honest way
Then still reach the top-without
Complete flop- of large and small and everything
Perilous times-perilous times
The kind that tests the all of all mankind.
With unrest all over the world
Female and male
All feel this tale
These kind's – this kind
Of time.

To Understand

When help is needed
To understand
What's not understood
In any way
With faith , ask the Creator
Night or day
Get help
Faithfully- the Eternal
Way , always.

Weather

Oceans drying
Icebergs melting
Warmer weather passing thru
Colder places getting warmer
Warmer places getting colder
Weather changing, people too
With many weather changes too-passing thru
Animals, people
Make changes too
Because – they,
Really, really
Have , to...thru changes in
Oceans, icebergs, weather too.

Thanksgiving

It's Thanksgiving time, but my wife's not here
With me this year
It's not quite the same as it was before.
Not quite the same this year.
But she's near in a
Convalescent home not far away
And I plan to be with her there
And have the holiday meal with her there today
And spend quality time with her there
In a very special way
It's a lot to be thankful in Creation's way that way
And show love to the
Creator to be with us.
Tho Thanksgiving's not quite the same.
My family and lot's of love is with me today
And that's lots to be thankful
For at this time... on,
Thanksgiving Day.

Someone

When someone is sick in the family
And it's someone real close to you
The days and the nights
Seem to speak , as they pass by
And flow right by you silent thru.
And they seem to say in a way
Just keep strong- Just keep strong,
Each day is just as before
Since time began- all this is part of a larger plan
You will soon understand
It is controlled and this had to be
It's being done all in love
As the heavens above
Just believe- like the flow of a beautiful stream
With the creation
And the one you care for will always be
Close, close, thru love
Your love which is strong – like hours are long
And they speak as they pass... To-
You and only you for you care deep
Deep like the stars in the Heavens above
With a love , and they understand
And feel as you do
And together in Creation
And together with love... all-
Will come thru as one.
Continue to do – with love
In love- Creation's love
As you've done.

Day

At the end of the day
Close the day
Rest-relax, your way
For you've learned, your way
And...
Start a new day.
It's the end –
Of the day.

Dark

A few days before Christmas- when there's
Illness around
In the wee hours of morning
When there's hardly a sound.
Save the formidable darkness
That seems to twitter it's way till on coming day
There's a comfort that seems to whisper in a way
And it comes it seems from a source
Few seem to know saying
Don't worry, all is ok – Believe trust in love
For I know
And my hours of dark- pass, more…
Quickly, till day, when-
There's illness around.

This Way

When friends come visit
From many years ago-and you all can think back
Then return to where you are today
It's both lovely and to, is quite beautiful.
For in a way you're saying
It's not being together and it's being together
That makes this possible.
And it's both beautiful and lovely
That it's done, in this way
Both years ago – and today.

Yuh - Say

Hey, yuh say
You got the world , by the tail
Hang on , hang on
It's a turnin- it's a turnin
Don't fall off- but if yuh do
Pick a soft spot to land
That'ul feel good,
When you're thru.

Seem

The higher and higher
And more high-you go
Some troubles, away
From you… seem
To flow.
Be careful
Don't stall the
Airplane, to high
Tho.

Remember

Some of what, you've told me
I'll remember
Some will pass me by
But when dream's come- and...
The part's mixed,
I remember-
Then , Then's – when I'll fly.

The Day

Today – is the day
To start- to do
One nice thing
For- some one else,
Everyday.
Today is the day.

All

Creation is wonderful
Creation is beautiful
Creation is lovely
From the smallest creature
To the highest mountain
To the deepest sea
Creation is wonderful
Creation is beautiful
Creation is lovely
And ...it is all,
There ever- will be.
The Creator
Made it that way
Creation is-
Wonderful, beautiful, lovely.

There

I went back to see- what used to be
And ... there were only
Two others there and me
But..
We left tracks to see.
Next time-with time
Only time
And the Creator
Will know –what's there –
To ever go back
To see.
But...I went back where
What used to be, to see.

School Day's

The folks that we know- in school day's
By name-remain
Close as the stars- tho they be far
As dark is from light
Yet in our sight
Where we feel, hear, touch-see
There they be.
Where we can thru memories
Be as-almost family.
The folks that- we knew
From those
Long ago…
School Day's.

The Time

Sunday mornings
Usually is
A day for you
To worship in a way
That's best for you
Do this in the way
You're accustomed too.
Sunday morning's or-
The time, for you-
This-to do.

Times

At times- we think
Oh my- we are, locked in
And panic may quickly
Then – set in.
But to act slow then
Think things thru
Creation helps
And… timely – freely –
See's us thru, think at times.

As Good

Do twice as good
With half as much
This sometime
Is the place
Folks find-They are
In-must
Move forward
From, and
Better do.
It's then…
They must gather
All at hand
At their command
Push-push-do,
Their very best
Keep well in touch
And…
Do twice as good, better too
With-
Half as much.

Of Quiet

Oh the thunderous
Selfish, quiet, permeating
Invasions of quiet.
That seek out and engulf you
Quietly- arouse you-
Tho –calming too
The quiet, the quiet
That's been here , since
And with Eternity
It's quite unseen- but…
Really beautiful too
The thunderous
Permeating quiet.

At Noon

To start your work at noon
Tis a strange time- to start at noon
Most have, half way finished
Their work – at noon
But if that's the way – work comes to you
Then work the way
Work comes, till thru
For when work comes at noon- then still
The time , for one to start
At noon- and do quite much….
There's, work to do
There's room.
At noon.

Dinner

We had dinner together- at church today
We ate together
We talked together- we laughed together
We had a good time together.
It seems there's magic that way
When folks are together
Have fun together, like when-
We had dinner at church today.

Keep

Put out the garbage, and the grass,
Keep in the sunshine – while it last's
Stay in the moonlight- starlight too
Keep on workin- till it's thru
But…
Put out out the garbage
And the grass
And…
Keep in the sunshine
While it last's.

Of Things

The mechanics of things
Just how things work
The mechanics of things
On this do not shirk- to get one ahead
So as not, to come up, sometime, dead.
The mechanics of things
Organization- organization
Must have this too- to get all the way thru
With good organization too
Then... you'll
Perhaps , maybe-
Slide thru.

Go Back

To go back and do
An unpleasant, past- passed thru
To wake up then...
A memory too
Is a something one
Most times not- but sometime
Must do- but... memories, seem to understand
And let one – this, pleasantly do
To go back, and wake up-
A memory too.
Memories most times-
Let's one this do.

To Me

I can remember
When as a child older folks
Their spouse
Would be called
Away
They then lived alone
I would see-to me
Their place then
Seemed kind of
Lonesome-strange.
I'm older now
It happened
To me
I understand why
As a child,
It seemed...
Kind of lonesome
Strange
Then-to me.

I remember.

Wonder

I wonder-I wonder
I wonder
Sometime, I do
How tomorrow
Tomorrow
The next day
The next-the next
Day, will be
Some time.
I wonder-I wonder
I wonder
Sometime,
I do
Do you?

Is Here

Good morning, good morning, the morning is here
I've stayed up all night
The morning is here
I've sat in my chair- and dozed the night away
In my recent- most three year way
I've stayed up all night
Good morning, good morning
The morning- is here.

Long Ago

Writing a book
Looking over pictures
Of long ago-of,
Your family tho
Children go,
This way-that way
As they grow.
Pictures tho…
Put back memories
In your mind
From pictures…
That you find
For the book,
That you are writing
Help-as you
Go-thru
The pictures-of…long ago.

Writing.

That Way

It might seem
Strange
But it happens sometime
Tho in it's way
It's kind
That you forget
What day of the week
It might be
And you think-and
Try to remember
But can't be sure
Especially if you're
Camping or by yourself
Sometime
You settle for the wrong day
Seems ok till
You find out it's not
At times-might seem
Strange
But it happens that way, still its ok.

24 Hours

Everyday
Every 24 hours
One complete day
One complete night
With…
Morning-noon-
Afternoon-twilight
Evening too
Is given free,
To everyone-
To use as you choose
Everyday
Every 24 hours.

Better

Together , together- grow better together
Grow stronger together
Grow loving together
Much better together
Than growing
Alone-
Much, better.

Can Be

Beautiful lovely
Can be too
In all we see
In all we do
If we let-
Beautiful lovely be,
Where- we, be
Under the sky
Of crystal blue
And sunlight too
Eternally.
Beautiful lovely
Can and always
With love, for free
Be there too.
And with us…
Go thru.

To Do

Revenge-revenge
A terrible thing to do
It reveals how the inner
Of the souls
Deep dark and inner feels.
Revenge-revenge
It speaks aloud
The inside feelings of
The one
That revenge
This does, this do
It comes back
Like the wind
That blows-
It haunts
Will forever
Bother you
Revenge-revenge
A terrible thing
To do.
To make peace
Is
Better
Much-much better
Vengeance
Is for…
The creator.

Thing's

Some things – that be
Are better left,
To
Their good or bad
Of – desired
In – memory
Some things..

Where

I'm looking in the mirror
You're standing right
Here too-yet…
I must say
I'm looking
In the mirror
And say,
Where are you?
I'm here-see me,
I know that
I see you
Yet…
You're not in
The mirror
Look yourself
I am…
And I don't see me.
Gosh-
Where did I go?

September

When September's
All finishcd
Soon Summer's
Gone
October's here-it's,
Cool dew
All around.
Then comes November
With Thanksgiving too
And December-
With snow on
The ground.
One looks for Spring
And Summer to arrive
With green grass
Green leaves
To see-that
Summer survived
After,
September arrived,

September.

Go

Go , go just go
How will I get there
Don't you know ?
You gotta be there ?
I don't know- I think so
Then … Just go
Go , go.

In Ways

Insects are small
But strong in ways
When they bite you
It stays and stays
They let you know
They came
Your way
And had of you
As they went-
On their way.
For…if they-bite you
It stays and stays,
Insects are small-
But strong, very strong
In way's.

116

The Time

Sunday mornings
Usually is
A day for you
To worship in a way
That's best for you
Do this in the way
You're accustomed too.
Sunday morning's or-
The time, for you-that's
This-to do.

Moves

What to do
From day to day
As life moves along
It's way
And you move too
In your own way
Each given, freely
Given day
Is all part of
Life's songs
In mostly lovely
Individual tones
From day to day
As life moves along
It's way and you move
Thru days, all must decide...this
Thru years-thru,
Doubts, love fears
In your own-very personal way, as-

Life...moves along.

Flew

I just seen a
Butterfly and a bee
Flying outside and
Landing on my
Tomato plants
And then they
Both-
Flew away.
I don't know where
The butterfly
And the bee went
They seemed happy
Maybe they were friends
The butterfly,
And the bee-as they
Flew away today.

Early

Early in the morning
When it's quiet all around- the dawn
With sun light, looks right at you
And smiles, with- good morning
With hardly any sound.
Early in the morning-
When it's quiet all around.

Working

To work-to work
Is wonderful
When years as-they flow
And working years go
Even volunteer work
Is quite different
On regular basis
To find.
And volunteer
Work is filled
Quickly most times
I write my style
Poetry, short
Stories, songs
To fill time
And find it keeps
Active my mind.
To work-to work
Is wonderful
To do
And work in
Some way
All that are able
Must do-their way
For that I'm quite
Sure is what
Creation expects
Us to do
In some honest
Way as long as
Creation permits
Us to on
The way thru.
To work-to work at
Honest work-we can do
Perhaps is what we're expected to do
Maybe-don't you
Think so too?

White Clouds

I see clouds
In the sky
Floating by in the sky
White clouds
In the sky
And the sky is blue
The drifting soft
Floating clouds
In the sky
Make a morning-
Beautiful beauty
In the bright blue
Sunshiny sky
I see clouds
In the sky
The clear blue crystal sky
I see white clouds-floating,
In the sky.

Together

One night- I waited up for midnight
Midnight came – and looked for me
I was so busy elsewhere, that midnight
I did not hear or see, so midnight went
To the very next day – and I went quick
To the other day too, along with midnight
Together – we went unknown, to each other-
Together and thru.

My Wife

A wonderful, wonderful woman
My wife-and
We were together
For years and years
A very good part
Of our lives
And happy
Happy most times,
Sometimes sad
Even then we tried
Before sunset
Those sad times
Each day- to put
Sad things away
For fifty eight
Years together
Were we
Children together
Family together
Home life, wonderful
Home life together
Travel together
Seen much of-
This country
Other countries
Together.
My wife has now
Been called away
By the creator
To stay.
But happy, happy
Together were we
For many, many years
A very good part
Of our lives

continues.....

That our family be-with,
That wonderful
Wonderful woman
That wonderful woman-
My wife.
How very, very
Fortunate
Were we, and I-
To be with that
Special lovely woman,
That woman-that woman
That woman…my wife.

What

What we see
That passeth by
What we hear
That missed the eye
What we touch
As years go by
Make us much
Of what we be
That we-and others
Touch, hear, see.
Also…
Help-blends
Grows-makes
Us be as we.
Now, how about that.

To See

In a room with
No windows or doors
That kind of room
The dark-
Adores, it's much as in a cave
Deep, deep inside
It is there
You'll find
That dark resides
On the ocean
Too where
There are no
Moon or stars
And it is night
The dark there too
Will be with you
Perhaps dark
Can come to stay
In either night
Or either day
If all is right
For dark
To come-
And be,
For you-
To see.

As in a room with-

No windows, or doors.

Noontime

Hands of the clock
Are moving
Round and round and
It is noontime now
The body's making
Noontime sounds
I hear body growls
Come now.
It's time to eat
A noontime meal
For the body
Would appeal.
Hands of the clock
Are moving
Round and round and
It is noontime now
It's time to eat. The clock,

The body agree– that's neat.

Play

Children, play- in a real fun way
Adults play- in a more careful way
Old folks play- in a very comfortable way
Everybody plays – in some kind of- way.

Give

The silence
Of the quiet
When alone-in dark of night
In a building
Or out too-
Gives the heavy
Tremendous heavy
Of the feeling
Of the quiet
Of the dark
Of alone
That feelings
Only feelings
Give-mixed
With haunting silence
That…
They do.
About you
Don't run from your true
Be true about
Your truth
About you
Don't run from it.
What you've done
Tell the facts
That's what folks
Want to hear about you
That's what folks
Want to know
About you.
Let chips fall
Where they may.
They may, anyway...for

Silence, quiet, time, tell-

Anyway.

Teenage

The teen age years
They with us go
They're always there
Where ever we be
They them we see
With memory
They kind of guide
Steer, silently
As years they build
And build and build-
As we grow and age
From thru that
Short page of
Learning teen,
Age years.
They kind of
With us go and in
Silence stay.
They're always there,
In…memory, the teen age years.

Birds Fly

Some birds fly- some birds don't
And some birds walk
When they're going by
Then – some birds swim
And then they fly, those seagulls do-
Way , Way – up high. Where birds they, fly.

Walking

There's a spider
Walking in my
Bathtub
There's no water
In the tub
But I don't like
Spiders
They have so many
Legs- moving
This way, that way
Sometime they might
Crawl on you,
Or-bite,
you.
Most of the time
They run away
I don't think spiders
Like either
Me or, maybe you
Right now tho
There's a spider
Walking in my
Bathtub, and...
I don't like spiders
Do you?

The Thing

A meal or gathering, just sets the tone
Of where or when – something
To be happened in the place
It's place, the thing
Or something will be,
In, it's part...
Of, history, just sets the tone.

Our Way

The telephone
Is usually silent
And very quiet, noisy-
Too
When one lives
Alone
All others gone
Grown-called
Away
And one is all
Alone.
Busy, busy one
Must keep,
And keep one's
Sanity too
So far I've found
Writing poetry, stories
Songs-reading-
Camping, I love camping
Helping others
Exercises too
Passes each days
Hours thru.
Tho-if
We think honest
And we must
If we think
In this way-the,
Silent and quiet, also noise
Is always there
For each of us
And comes at
Creations given
Days-as we
Pass thru
On, Our way, kind of

Like the telephone.

Everywhere

To hear them
Walking
And they're not there
To hear them
Talking
And they're not there
To hear them
Whispering
And they're not there
To hear them
Whistling
And they're not there
To hear them
Shrieking like a banshee
And they're not there
You look close
You hear-see
They move things
But they're not there
It's the wind,
No one can see it-
But it's there-its everywhere.

The Moon

Went outside
The moon was shining it,
lit tonight.
The world almost like day
But the moonlight light
looked like
Moonlight light
not like
daylight light
in the day.
When I went outside
And the moon was
Shining tonight.

Choice

To be the first
To be the last
A choice that's made
To last-must start
Small and low
And build
To show
From small
The all
Thru to large
That grows
And grows-suffers
With times
And loved as true
From love
That true
And honesty
From last-to first
A choice and-
Followed true
Weak to strong
Last to first
Leads its way
Honestly thru
Belief thru
To-a last-
To…a first.

And thru.

Earth

Like an island
In the sky
The Earth…
Rotates, rotates, rotates-
In the sky, like an island.

Minister

To have been
Picked
By the creator
To minister-or
Teach and influence
Spiritual in
Spiritual ways
For days-years
Is a blessing
Eternal-blessings
That's lovely
With-creations,
True love. To have for this

Been picked.

Spoke

I spoke to my cat
In my language
She answered
Don't know-if she understood
For sure
But she seemed to
She seemed to for sure
Maybe I can speak
A little cat language
Don't know about that
But I just spoke
To my cat
And she answered
for food.
And no more
Cats are here, for sure-
Their relation too.
Been here- will be here
For days-cat ways
And many-
Years thru. I, just spoke to her.

Went Away

They're still hanging
There-where you
Left them-when
You went away
All your clothes…
I see them everyday
And touch them
Sometime
They have memories
Surprisingly strong
After years long
Past gone since
You wore them
Memories
Strong-even
Today, they do
They're still hanging
All your clothes
Where you left them
When, you went away.

Please

You're welcome
You're welcome
Like the notes
Of a song
When the notes
Move away-
Please- move
Along, Thank you

Plant

A plant that help's
In sickness much
It's proved to many
It's magical touch
Is refused to-
The many, by some
Of few
By belief it could
Damage some belief
Of the few.
A plant that helps
In sickness much
If refused to many
By some of the few.
Now, is that something,
Good to do? Some think so, some do.

Lesson

Missed my lesson
Yesterday
Thought about it
Anyway
Missing lessons
Has a way
To kind of smudgen
Up the day.
But spite of everything
And all-here tis today
Missed my lesson yesterday
Thought about it
Anyway.

Feed

Feed the cat and feed the dog
Feed your animals too
And think of all, the company
They give you –
As you feed the cat- and feed the dog
And feed your animals
Too..

We You, They Do

You speak the language
That you do
You meet someone that
Does not to-speak the language
That you do
You two marry that you do
And have a family
That speaks and understands
The both of you
And speaks some of
The language of the
Both of you
And other families do the same
As what your family does
That's what they do
To make a place
Of what we see
And hear
In what we do
In many places
That we do.

Speak..languages.

Wonderful

To change the way one
See's a cloudy day
There's blue in the sky
And sunshine too
As clouds drift by
Then sunshine's thru
To change the way – one
See's dark of night
There's moon with mystery
To light night as history
And stars there with story
Of centuries – their glory
Many times
Ones out look, gazed, took
With most little
Of silent, change
The simply – just
Wonderful, brings...

To change.

Clock and Picture

Tho,
You stay in a room
With a clock
On the wall
And a picture too
The clocks hands move
And the picture
Watches you
The clocks hands move
And seem to watch
Sunrise – sunset each day
In a strange, strange way
While the picture
Glares too
In a peculiar way
They both are your friends
In their own
Way tho
The clock on the wall
And the picture
Too
As they both stay,
In the room-
With you.

The Sun

The sun comes up in the morning-
Over the mountain tops
Travels past, where the moon is in the sky.
To the top of the world- where
Noon time is – possibly,
Thru twilight, evening- drops
To mountain tops
On the worlds other side and resides
Thru night each day-
After morning … in the sky
When the sun comes up .

Leaf

The Tree was green
One leaf fell down
The other leaves stayed
Maybe they thought
When the tree – is thru with me
I probably too
Will have to fall, fall down
Maybe – in their way
Leaves think
Maybe…
Do you think they do?

Talk

Lets talk about
What we never
Talk about
For we really want
To hear what
We never talk about
Why do we never
Talk about it
Anyway
We want to know
About it
Why is it kept away
We want to know
About it more
Everyday
Lets talk openly
About that what
We never talk
About that's
Within us –
Ok and…
And how about today.
Sounds good, lets talk.

Eleven Dollars

I'm big and I'm nine and I saved
My allowance too
I've got eleven dollars Mom told me –
We could go to the mall
Mom knows – I just love to go there, and just
Look and look there at all the really
Really neat things there
Especially , with my Mom
I'll take some of some of the bunch
Of money I've saved with me – and have
Oh, so much fun- just Mom and me
I'll get something nice real-real nice, to share
With Mom and my brother- and me
With some of my eleven dollars
I've saved-when I go to the mall
Mom and me – gosh- Gee whiz-Za- wee.
It's sure nice – to be big and nine
Saved your money –go shop at the mall
With your Mom too
Mom and I just-
Walk and walk , and walk there till we're thru
I'm so happy-gosh….
Lucky, lucky me. I'm big,

And I'm nine.

Chimney Top

I see pigeons today, flying in the air
Flying, flying, flying
To most everywhere
Some stop on my- neighbors
Chimney top I guess
Because it's up high there
And they can see
All over- and feel safe
There, on the chimney top –
When they stop,
I see pigeons- I see pigeons
Today.

Evening Comes

When evening comes, and night
With dark ,with moon, will soon
Fill the sky
Birds , of the day –fast go away
To rest, till sun
The next day, will again- fill the sky.

People

When the weather is nice
People like to have
Picnics
And parties too
People have picnics
And parties
Lots of people
Do, when-

The weather, is nice.

For Free

A building
A building
A building
For free – for you
And me – to live
Explore
With the sky
For a ceiling the north – south
East, west
For walls, windows
Door's
The earth for
A floor
That building
A building
a building
a building – that building
is free – for you
for me
to live – for free
and…
to, always
Explore, its-

The…earth.

Just Be

Be you – be you
Don't be a slave
Don't be a phony
Just be you
Be of the few – be of
The few
Just be you
Never ever be a slave
To anything
They don't have of good
A ring
And don't be a phony
Just be you, plain old you-old you. Be you

Stories

Stories make
Our histories
Then others read
The histories
And make more
Good stories too
Stories and
Histories too
Why, I'm sure –
They'll just,
Never, ever…
Stop, going
Thru,

Stories.

Thought

Thought
I kind of thought
We would be together here forever,
But time didn't think
That should be
For all changed thru the years
That has to be, everyone grows
Moves on – has to be share
Times, grow with time and
It seems for all even –
To-tal-ly, just appear to leave
With time children grow
Move on , have family
Houses bedrooms they empty-
Parents at home only two, then- and,
As grandparents too
With grandchildren passing thru.
And time as it kind of
Maybe its way perhaps
Takes one at that ones given day away
Never to return- no never- its forever.
Creations way
Its I guess creations way
Of explaining in a solemn way
That may be. To be happy
Lovely happy together everyday
With love and understanding
Creations way – as everyday
Tends to pass thru
Stay , love , trust ,each other-
For together all are…
In, a– way
Creations way.

Days

The days they just , seem to
Meander by
I – at times wonder too
Do the days in some way
Watch you
And wonder why
That you, who are you
Why do you,
Also-
Watch them too
As they pass
Day by day, every day-
Thru– the days, those days.

Paranoid

The sky might fall- The sky might fall
The ocean might run over too
Fill everything with water
So nothing more can move thru.
Mountains might slide
Turn the earth to one side
Might happen, could happen too.
Are you paranoid ?
No …
But I watch for marbles,
When walking so as
Not to fall.
The sky might fall
The sky might fall
The ocean might run over too.

The Magnet

I could climb mountains
I could soar stars
I could walk deserts
I could go far
I could swim rivers
Go over waterfalls too
There isn't much I wouldn't go thru
But I can't – you're not there
You're the magnet that
Pulls- like a strong golden hair
A light thru the dark-that beams-
And you're there.
And isn't it strange
Quite like a rainbow too
You've always been there
You've helped pull me thru
So now the mountains to climb-
The stars-rivers too
I still can do.
If you in my memories
Will stroll with me , thru.

Quiet

The house was all quiet
Cause no one was there
They told me you sleep
But sleep wasn't there- the quiet is noisy.
There thunder abounds
It tramps thru the quiet
And makes it's own sounds
It bothers your brain
Quite like springtime rain
But not in a beautiful way
And quiet is quiet and when you see thru
There's love in the quiet
That's strong- moves away
Bothersome things
Bringing soothing love
That's lovely with sleep
You'll feel that's
Just for you- to help; you thru.

Listen

Silence is golden
And memories are too
The wind, the leaves, the branches,
The waves, the tides as they
Crash on ever awaiting shores,
And our friends as they speak
As we listen them thru.
Creation is… silent- thunderous
Lovely golden too
As we speak- it listens, listens, waits,
Momentarily
As it tiptoes- quietly
Soft, flowing-
Thru.

Flying

Oh, that bird flying low
So it can see-
Everything on the ground
Below
Sometime birds
Fly high
Sometime birds
Fly low
So they can better see
All that they can see
On the ground
Below.
That bird is flying low.

The Night

The stars they light like banners the night
The moon there too, it lights as one- the night
Together the stars, the moon…light night
With mysterious light
That lights with love most earth at night
With Heavenly
Starlight and moonlight.

Hours

The hours, they move quiet- going by
Like clouds move in the sky
I think maybe – the sun, it watches
Tho… when it brings night-
As it sets low, in the sky.
So all, will know
The hours – have passed
Quiet, by.

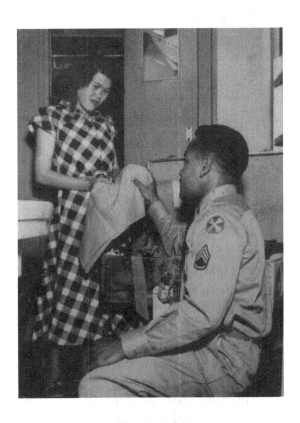

The Years

You liked what I liked
I liked what you liked
Mostly you did what I did
Mostly I did what you did
We talked things thru- most times
Before the sun was thru
Or before the sun went down
The best way to end the day
You understood what I understood
I went where you went
You went where I went
We understood in our way
The years passed by, a happy way.
We're happy now, in our own way
I guess we done
We did what we done
We're not done yet
And we done it together- with love
And we done it, thru

The years.

Yesterday

Yesterday… came with the sun and-
Stayed with the sun, all day
And when-
The sun went away the day-
Went away too.
But …
I still remember, yesterday some
And the sun-
When yesterday… went thru.

Go

I go to church
I sit, I listen, I sing commune
And when- the church is thru
I go- home.
Roam , thru the days- with the days-
Of church, of thoughts, my ways
Hours, days, more days-
All week, and … pass years, this way – thru.

With church as company, too.

The Day

When you-
Stay up late, if that's your way
You miss most of the day, next day
Because night comes along
Like the notes of a song
And takes your short day right away
So – if you,
Stay up late if that's your way
You miss, most of a
Big part of
Your very next day.

You do.

Large Way

Isn't it odd-in kind of
A great large way
That the dirt-we walk on
Live on, thrive on
Exist on, build on
Fight, leave, return to
In some form
Love on-learn on
Die on-go back to
Is always
The very same dirt
We came from
In many ways, everything
Over and with time
Just coming, living, learning
Going back to dirt
Isn't it odd-in kind of
A great large-hard to really
Understand but true way
of course– tho,
it's creations way
and all…all-
must do.

Six Pm

To awake at six pm, a six pm-
Breakfast, in a day is still breakfast
It's way it adds breakfast to the day.
As evening slides thru
With night coming too- your way.
Soon after – a six pm
Breakfast in a day
It's the way – tho… to awake at six pm
For eating breakfast.

Slidin Along

Ailments – we've all got some kind, untold
Both the young , and yes the old
But we move right on thru life
Don't have time for minor strife.
Life goes on- and we go too
Have to, in order to get thru.
Most are happy, seems they be
Takin whatever ailments be… day by day
Come what may- hummin, singin, lifes song
Each quite differently – slidin… along.

Your Way

One should do- what you can do
That is good to do, each day
Or you may wish, that you did do all - that you
Could do each day
By then it's probably to late to do what
You didn't do, today
So … think good, of good
That you can do, and do the good
Another day-
Your way.

No Other Way

The world moves forward
Inch by inch
There is no other way
We move forward usually
Slowly – it seems
There is no other way
If we move too fast
We lose our way – it seems
There is no other way
When we read a book
We understand – that what
We want to see it seems
There is no other way
In the light of the sun
We see – mainly what we
Want to see – it seems there
Is no other way
Causing the world
To move forward inch by inch
It seems –
There is no other way.

Where

Up, where the sky is blue
Where the sun and moon stay too
That's where we would like to go
But it is so high
We could never go- and come back to tell
Because it is so high
Way up in the sky- way out,
Where the sky is blue
And the sun and moon-
Stay too.

Unless

Relationships – relationships,
They cause, build and destroy creation too,
Unless we build them thru love
In some way too
For only thru love- can relationships
Do the all…
They are supposed to do.

Like That

When a song – or a poem
Or something, like that
Comes to you, write it down then- because
When things come to you , like that-
They hardly ever , come back again,
Maybe…that's why,
They came to you, perhaps… for, you.

That, song or poem or-

Something like that.

Season

The season of the now we see
And the way it comes
Wherever we may be
So beautifully
In memories and with actuality
With young and old
Also in gifts of eternal lively
Very own and equally blend
Thru the season of the now
We see the beautiful Christmas season
The lovely Christmas eve right now
A beautiful and eternal Christmas
Soon very soon
With many blessings blending smoothly
In silence
As sun, moon, stars
And comes to each with a special
Very special blessing felt with others
Thru the creators love
The season of the now we see, Christmas

Say

Say…Look- look-look
Up in the sky, I can see
An elephant, a horse, a fish, a mountain go by
Look what the clouds make for you-
To see, high up in the sky?
As they drift , slow, high, silent- by.

Look-look...look, up in the sky.

Pasture

When the horse is old- it's put in the pasture
Where life there and all there- as the seasons
With the seasons comes , and grows, and goes-
Like the seasons.
When the horse is old it's put,
In the pasture … the pasture wait's.

Sail On

Sail on- sail on, sail on, with life, each day
Get on in the morning , sail thru morning –
To noon , afternoon too- thru twilight,
Evening to bedtime – sail thru bedtime
Thru sleep- to dawn, morning too-
Sail on , with life each day
Sail on- sail on , sail on
That's the way … thru.

Tides

Our lives maybe
Kind of in a way
Like the tides of an
Ocean moves its way
The good given out
Come back slow in
Someway.
The bad given out
Does so too in
Its way
And this action
Continues
Life times thru
Our lives maybe
Like or similar
To the tides of
The ocean with…
The good bad we do
Going-returning
Life time's-
Thru.

Anytime

School time, studytime, worktime, sleeptime
Anytime- all the time
Time has something for you to do.
All you have to do – is go look-
And .. get busy too, anytime.

Given

Sunday, worship day- learn to do good day
Monday thru Saturday weekdays-
Workdays –days to do good- bad things-
Too , days.
Sunday again – worship day, self check day
On good , bad done-
On week days, work days
Days , days, - we're all
Given, days.

I Forget

If I think, and think
And think about
That I was thinking about
What I forgot
Will come to me
If I keep
Thinking about
What I forgot about
If I can
Remember enough about it
To think about
What I was thinking about
And…
Think and think about it
Maybe, what I forgot
Will come
To me-
Maybe.

Same

Grass and trees of green-are much the same
Ocean's and rivers - of waters are same-
Only oceans have salt rivers have none.
The sky-with beautiful blue by day-
Deep blue by night-in Heaven high
Are always of beauty the same
Sun, moon, stars- gentle breezes
The winds of beauty-they are too
Of much the same, as move they do,
With silence thru … Tho, much of silence is of same
To us- as we… move of swift,
And thru.

Of much-is nearly, same.

In Town

When the rain man comes
It rains in town- when the snow man comes
It snows in town
When the sunshine comes
And the sunshine's round
The other men leave
Cause it's warm in town- it's warm in town
It's warm in town- it's warm in town
The snow man leaves, the rain man leaves
Cause, its warm in town – it's warm in town
It's warm in town
Those men … they leave …
Cause – it's warm in town- it's warm in town

Beautiful

How beautifully beautifully
Beautiful
The beautiful of beauty
Can be
In the beautiful of mountain valleys
Filled with green
Far away distantly near
Mid hazy blue of trees
As one moves
Thru all this beauty
With extreme exquisite
Care
One can sip
Lightly
On natures
Just natural
Beauty to be found
Waiting there
Waiting always waiting
Always…
Waiting there.

Thinking

Traveling by thinking's
Good to do-
Ox carts oxen
Horses buggies
Too
Bicycles cars
Trucks, they'll do
Trains airplanes
Get you there
Too
Walking, skateboards
Now that's a way
Too
Sailboats, ships
Submarines, they'll do
Balloon's too-
But, imagination's
The quick way.
Traveling by thinking's…
Good to do.

A Ride

A bicycle ride, near the end of the day
When the sun – has passed
Over halfway, mark in the sky
Is just a wonderful way to kind of
Watch the rest of a day pass by
A bicycle ride … take a bicycle ride,
Near the end of the day.

Roll

Bicycles roll, skateboards, cars, trains, buses
Some chairs too, and - roller skates, with whesls
On their heels do- but cats dogs-
And people, they – don't roll
They … walk thru.

A Treat

To eat, and feel good- it's a treat
To do that , just to eat – be able to,
And do that … when you do
It's a treat, just to eat
It's a treat-a blessing too
It is,
Really … it is.

Hot

When the weather
Is really, really
Hot
Where most of
The time
It is not
Folks behave in
A very different
Way
Than they most
Times do.
By saying when-you meet,
It sure is really,
Really, really hot
Today and most stay-
More inside.
When the weather
Is really, really hot
Where most of the time
It is not.

Toilets

Toilets, toilets, toilets
They are everywhere you go
Babies use diapers- most animals use the ground
Anywhere around- flies they use windows,
Anyplace they be- fish they use the water
People special little rooms
In homes or places for toilets
Toilets, toilets, toilets
They are everywhere for most everything
Everywhere , you go.

Fly

The airplanes fly, oh so noisy, in the sky
The bees, the mosquitoes,
The flies do too, the birds some sing
But most fly very quiet – in the sky
Also kites- they fly, but with a string in the sky.
Tho…
Airplanes fly noisy in the sky,
Airplanes fly, very , very high.

Lights

Lights , lights-we must have light
There is, sunlight, moonlight, starlight too.
Buses, cars, trains, boat, bicycles, homes
Hospitals, with lights
People carry flashlights too
Lights, lights, lights
We must have light.

An Evening View

There's clouds low on the
Mountains around
And lights are
Coming on in
The houses around
Here also its
Near sunset
Almost dark damp
Too after a
Recent rain
Giving this campground
Where I'm camping
Writing too
And I think
An almost dark
Sunset different
Cloudy mountain
Too
Kind of late evening
View with
Clouds low on the mountains
Around
Always house lights, they're-
Coming on, and the view
Is quite a nice late, evening view.

Weather

Nice days, nice days, not too hot-
And humid too-make nice days
Special days- and make you like
That kind of weather too
Those kind of nice days
Nice days do.

Alone

Holidays are different
When you spend them
All alone
They fill the home
With different
Kind of cheer
Its sort of – kind of
Wishing . hoping
Days would finish
Hurry get to
Ending,
Of the year
Of course
The new years days
Are much the same
Only holidays
Are supposed too
Give a different
Feeling when,
More than one
Is there
With only one
There's that
Half full – half empty
Almost nothing
Holiday feeling
Of now lets,
How lets,
Do we
Get this
Back to
How it was before
With the love
That's missing
Tho its inside
Deep, deep, deep
We feel kind
Of empty
All alone.

Still

Little red wagon
Even painted blue
It's still the little red wagon
That…
Children love,
Too
The little red wagon.

Peacock School 1934

To Do

It's lovely to watch ,the seasons go thru
Creation knows just what to do
How to bring all the seasons
Just beautifully thru
It's so lovely to watch-
The seasons go thru.

.

Each Day

At sunset each day
And at sunrise too- each day comes
With love for everyone, even- you
Did you know that ?
Now ain't that nice
All that fuss- for us, just us
Each day … but the world, was made,
That way, for everyone, everyday-

And, that's nice. Each, day.

The Beach

Go down to the beach today
Stroll the beach-where the starfish lay.
Where the waves touch the beach then-
Go back far
Walk the beach- leave tracks in the sand
Walk far, then come back again
Gaze far out over the ocean
Where the blue of the sky-touch
Ocean waves nearby.
Go down to the ocean today-
Stroll the beach, where the starfish lay.

A Picture

Take a picture of –
A little Japanese Maple tree
With leaves of golden green
All mixed with reddish red.
It stands in the corner of a fence-
And lives in brown of sand,
Where children play, everyday.
Take a picture of this little maple tree,
With leaves of Golden Green
All mixed with reddish red.
The tree … was planted for my wife-
When she left,
It means a lot to me. The picture, will too.

All Mine

Look at this- all thru and thru
I bought it, I bought it, it's all mine too
And when I am- thru with it
Or … tired of it- I can break it,
I can keep it, I can give it away
Any time- any old day, because-
Look at this all thru and thru,
I bought it- I bought it
It's all mine too.

All Day

A mouse- is a mouse in the house
All day, and when it hears a noise-
It runs away, and when every things quiet
It comes back again
Then eats and plays- really has
Great fun again,
Just being … a mouse, in the house all day.

Playtime Sometime

Play in the sunshine- play in the sand
Play in the water
In the moonlight too
Play, play- most any old time
Play, play laugh and play
It's healthy- it's, good for you
To play- anytime sometime too.

Season's

The cold of winter- the blossoms
And green of spring- the rains where birds
Even the Crane is seen in spring
And summer
Oh , the warm of summer
Like warm friendship- friends bring
Memories too
The sunrise, the moonlight, and all to remember
From the season of – winter
Of spring- summer – friends
Memories over years of long, of slow
Like the walk, of a turtle might go.
Like seasons of slow, few, more, new too.
And all seem to bring-
A something beautiful-as they move
Memorably, anciently- eternally-
Of then … thru,
Like gifts sent
all lovely beautiful- thoughtful…
Also
the most lovely, lengthy,
Beautiful , Happy , Days , Years, always.
Traveling, traveling, thru,
Come,
With...the seasons, the seasons,
The...seasons.

On The Way

When the day's all finished
And the sun's put away
And the moon climbs slow – in the sky-
It's way, and the birds of the day,
Get all quiet their way
And dark tells evening quietly-
Very quietly- night time, is …
On the way
It's time to relax- for
The day's all finished, soon-
Tomorrow's , here to stay.

Make

Help, make the weakest strong
So strong all together help
Keep all strong.
Also …
Make the weakest strong.

Share

Age turns a page- unseen but felt
As a wind , brisk- of storm.
That gives strong alarm
Of a special day, in an alarming way
That's known to all it concern's
To be aware – a curve has been turned
Proceed on- but with care
A page of age has
Been turned- for you, to share.

Is

Tell Me,
Is what is   - is
Is what I see,   is
Is what I hear, is
Is what they say, is
Is what I think, is
Just what really is, is
And if you see, is
Tell me,
Also…and,
Tell is - Hi.

A Tree

An enormous tree fell
In the forest- one day
And no one was near –to hear,
The tree fall, when it fell that day
Except, the birds, and a bee,
And a full moon- nearby
The great tree was tall, very high
Many years – it spent
Reaching , toward the sky
And no one to tell- nor to hear
The tremendous sound … but-
The birds, a bee, and a full moon nearby
When if fell, from so high
While …
Reaching- reaching, reaching…
Toward , the sky.

That enormous, tree fell.

Now

Stop , stop, stop and listen now
Your ears might- not believe
If they could only hear
What you are saying, stop, stop, stop
Please, stop and listen now.

Words

Careful – careful,
With- words, words, words
They hit hard-
Just like a fist, and if heard
Very seldom – do they miss
So with words … be,
Careful, careful, careful,
Because , words … don't go home
Like pigeon's do- they roam and roam
They're … never thru.
Careful, careful,
Be careful-be careful
With words.

Punctuation

When you write- or when you wrote
When you mark, what did you write ?
If you mark, and did it right
If you mark , and did it wrong
Using punctuation
You might be in a different situation
You might have … made a letter, a poem
Mistake – or, perhaps, a song
Punctuation , punctuation- makes a different
Situation to what you write- of what you thought
That you did write, now- wow how about that
For the , old, write- wrote- written to say
When you write- what did you write ?

A Shadow

A shadow just moved by on my
Patio floor and … I think
A bird flew by
And maybe … made the shadow
That moved – on the floor.
Shadows move, quietly ,silently, by-
Like clouds floating … in clear blue, of sky.

Years Spent

The years we spent together
They come as a book to me-
Thru my memory, I can see them
As thru crystal clear of water-
In clear, smooth, soft flowing brooks
And they seem to speak, too-
In a kind of loving way- that recalls
The lovely years – we spent together
Before you were called away-
Yes …
The years we spent together
In our own, just- lovely , yet …
Most , memorable ways.

Those years– those lovely years.

Won

What have you won
In what you've done,
And , did… was that you,
Should not have done- what you done
In what you've done.
Really now… What have you won
Now this is done- have you won ?

A Shadow

A shadow just moved by on my
Patio floor and … I think
A bird flew by
And maybe … made the shadow
That moved – on the floor.
Shadows move, quietly ,silently, by-
Like clouds floating … in clear blue, of sky.
When the midnight is gone
And it's 2 or 3 hours past or maybe,
The hours of four before dawn
As dark moves along.
Little light tappings in the night
Of the lonely , of the lonesome
Unseen, unknown- but make their
Presence known- of light that's all right
That's ok for you're alone- where you be
Noises help you feel, tho not see, that ..
This in a way is company, as a shadow-
Till dawn of day, and goes away,
When midnight is gone
And it's 2 or 3 hours past or maybe
the hours of four before dawn, that's ok
Shadows sometime have noisy friends.

Something

Angry , angry, angry- about something
I didn't do , you're here so…
I'm angry at you too
You don't know why –I'm angry at you
And neither do I
But … I'm angry, angry, angry
About something – I didn't do
My angry will pass soon – pass thru
Stay, hope you'll stay
Please do

Unseen

I can see two trees- moving, moving
Swaying, swaying this way, that way
Then they motionless stop, stop's way
I see the trees- and the wind- Tho… unseen,
Makes the trees to move, to sway
I see two people moving , moving
Going, swaying- stopping too, in their way
As they move thru- something deep within
Unseen cause's people to move their way
I see trees and people moving ,swaying-
Stopping from the unseen- this I see most
Everyday and most times, from the quietly
Silently ,unseen – in, it's way.

Maybe

Sometime at times perhaps-
Maybe it's nice – to be , where
We imaginary, imagine
And cause , our minds to be
Then …
Come back to reality.
Maybe- Maybe.

Help

Love, how does it help, what does love do ?
Why is love needed, as seeds from the ground.
Or all around
Is love a phantom- that stays as notes
From a song sung ?
Why is love around as a scar of
Admiration from a beautiful lovely star.
What does love do, what has it done
How does it help and in what way, thru-
The days love seems to mean much, to each-
In different ways- thru experiences of life
Thru good or strife, that gives hope
Security contentment for comfort of good
That is good to each in lovely ways of memories.
Beautifully, eternally, beautiful too as we
Pass thru… Love helps much – in all we do.

Songs

Singin in the evening
Strummin singin songs
Singin with the guitar
Singin singin songs
Singin in the evening
Singin strummin songs
Singin with the guitar
Wherever you are- singin in the evening
Moves in a nice way
Moves the night along
Singin in the evening
Just, singin, singin, songs

Spins.

The world still spins- little things
That happen along the way
Learn from them- make better days
The world still spins- to let you thru
And you too, can win
Cause…
While the world it spins
It looks, For… and-
Expects – you too.

By Oneself

Living by oneself
In a house all alone –with no one
But yourself- is quite the same
As being – all alone
On an island or a star- off far,
If a decision you make
It's a chance you take
There's none to talk to
To decide anything with you.
If you leave, when you go –
When to return there too
There's none to decide there with you
What you do.
Living by oneself in a house
All alone when at one time there
Were for many years, two.
Is an experience in life, perhaps…
Many experience, thru.

Experience.

World

In your world- it's not the same as mine
You see things that aren't the same
As those, in mine
I see things in my world that you don't see
Our worlds have much different we can see
And if both worlds together
Your world, my world we can see
Think of all the beautiful we can see
Because …
Your world is not the same as mine
Our worlds are worlds of different kinds

Tunnel's

When you sometime feel- there's no one there
In the tunnel with you, don't stop-keep on
Like rabbits, when they hop
Keep on thru- to the light
There you'll find, birds that fly, find light there
The new to try, and others there to reason with
When for you, sometime their need, you need
These tunnels, may give –
For you … to you. Keep on, and thru.

Memories

It happened – it happened
I seen it happen to others
And I helped them thru
I don't know why, that for some
Reason when it happened to others
I just thought what would I do if-
Sometime this happens to me.
And then it did, you were called away
On that special day – after all the years
58 nearly 60 years- we were together
You were called away
I will never forget our years Creation
Gave us together- the family-
The lovely together, it was beautiful
It was lovely-we had our trials
Our good , bad times, but we went thru
All together- thru most everything
Not agreed on, before usually, before
Daily sundown, or sunset settled in.
The beauty of the new day then,
Showed Creations love a new way-
Which we found to be always more beautiful
Thru the days that way.
I thought it would never happen to me
When you went away
But the Creator called you away
My friends-our family helped ,and I
Could feel your presence your love/
Which always surrounds like sunshine,

Moonlight, star light, surrounds with help
Thru the days in loving ways.
I thought it never would happen
But it did- I feel that we are
Together thru memories
And memories are lovely
Beautiful-in special ways, thru giving…
Of light given-
Each given day, much
In-

Continues...

continues ...Memories

Eternal memorable ways
And giving,
All that happens
With love- of past
Also now, also before
Of the new, of ways, and more- thru
Understanding, offered
Of … also sprinkled lightly
With, the days. As life happens.

Planted

The little tomatoes plants, I planted
This year just grew, and grew
Little delicious- red tomatoes
I shared some with
My neighbors and used them
For salads too
The tomatoe plants I planted this
Year just grew ,and grew , and grew

Seems So

Shadows seem to get longer
Longer everyday
Along about sunset, it's way
Down toward the hills
And the mountaintops
In the near and faraway
Everyday …
It seems- so that way.

Shadows seem to get longer.

Comfortable

Resting, resting, resting
Resting in the sunshine
I see my old cat- resting-sleeping
Comfortable- in the sunshine
And I thnk, that's what
Most cats like, to do
Rest and sleep-
Out in the sunshine.

Class

Attended a class yesterday,
For we older folks that drive to,
Discover and see things we've
Developed unintentionally-
Methods we've made, of our kind
Over time ,that we thought was ok
In our driving- that don't work well
In modern days,
That we could, should, and must change
To safely drive in today's society
And safely stay, behind the wheel
And deal with the flow and with
Traffic be safe to go.
We also learned to soon consider
Other ways of transportation to get
Us to our destination
Because …
That today happens to all as we,
Aging with year's- get, and
Over time all, must do
For safety
Per- m- nent- ly
Tho one usually,
Does- this ,,, very-
Re- luc- tant- ly.
We learned much in our
Class yesterday about,
Driving , aging, accepting,
Blending , and … society
It-
Was a good class- tho.

For we...of yesterday.

149

Money

We all want money
Gimmie your money, Honey
Gimmie your money
Money-money.
Gimmie " all " a your money
And … thank ya stupid cause-
We all want money- don't you too ?
Gimmie your money –
" All " a your money.

Of Us

Obesity- obesity, it comes with us
And lives with us- it makes itself
A real part of us, in what we eat
In what we do
And creeps in silence
Right in with us ,is hard
Real hard to make leave from us
In young, old, middle age too
It likes very much to be a part of us
Obesity-obesity
It likes very much, all of us
And wants to be, and is in-
A big, big, very big – part of us, obesity.

Started

We met again- in Kobe Japan
Many, many years ago
And started a life that would
Stretch in it's way for many days,
Years, too that would show thru
Time understanding, patience just
What time- understanding, patience-
Love family altogether mixed
Just lovely with and thru the years
Together could and would do
We found again I must say –together
All mixed with family, we found the
Lovely filled with lasting love that
Was felt beautifully lovely as memorable
As a Rainbow at twilight- Opening
A door to a Golden , radiant tomorrow
We felt that way when and since we
Met that day in Kobe Japan .
Tho the one I met that day was or has
Been called away, by the Creator, to stay
I still, believe there always will be the
Bond of colorful, lovely with memories
Beautiful- as a rainbow at twilight,
Of and from our having met, arranged-
By the Creator. When we met again.

Moving Hand

The moving hand, having writ
Moves on to other writing,
Sighting, something of new
For writing.
The moving hand moves, moves on
Always on- seeking writing,
Having writ- writing …
,Writing, always new, the moving-
Hand moves on, on … to new.

Harvest

When it's Autumn in the country
And the leaves begin to fall
When things growing in fields,
For harvest like grains, fruit and such-
Are ready, then's the time folk's
On farms are really busy- gathering in
The crops that grew. when its Autumn
In the country, and leaves, begin to fall.

I Think

If you think, the sky is blue
If you think- the ocean's deep
If you think-that grass is green
If you think the sun is far
If you think the moon is far
If you think a star is too
Then you think
Like- I do …
And many others-
I , think too.

Orchid Flower

I bumped the little flower the little
Orchid flower
Given in my wifes memory.
I so carefully grew, near my living
Room door- I bumped the little flower
Accidently and it fell softly to the floor
I will watch closely to see if another
Orchid flower grows on that stem.
My wife liked orchid flowers and most
Always kept some of them. I just accidently
Bumped the little flower and broke it from the
Stem- new buds now stay. Watched everyday.

A Wonderful Thing

To talk- to talk
Is a wonderful thing
It's a wonderful thing just to talk
Why it is almost- like
A lovely walk, out in the brilliant-
Sun where one gets much
Needed exercise done.
To talk- to talk
To be able to talk
Is a wonderful ,
Most wonderful thing- just to talk.

151

To Say

With full attention the listener must
Listen to what the speaker has to say
In the message of the day. For full
Listening has a way to bring the
Message full the speaker desires
To convey, and in full, its meaning.
So listen, listen fully listen-
To what- speakers in their way
Has to say.

Everywhere

Sunlight shines the same most everywhere
On the mountains- on the valley's
On the hill's and flat lands too
It shines and when it does
It covers areas- thru and thru
Dark of night it does the same
Covers all equally the same
Good and bad they cover too
Sunlight- night generous are they for
They come free
Thru creation to feel to see
Thru faith-
For you and me.

Most Gone

The sunshine near the end of the year
When summers- most gone, and
Autumns near here, the light of the
Sunshine seems different nearby and
Warm, friendly warmer.
As some birds flies away others slowly
Leaving. trees changing colors, for cool
Of Autumn's close by- with the sunshine
Differently near… it seems.
It's soon- the end-
Of, the year.

Words

To write the words in red- to write
The words – in green to write
The words in black or blue
To write the words once written
If all the words are new
To write the words
To write the words
The words, if the words are new
And seen
It matters not if words
Are in red- or black
Or blue- or green.

Perhaps

Once a work is completed
Done your best and in your way
Perhaps- it's best to step back close
The door and move away
Work again another place
Do your best- and in your way
With memories, just look back …
For once the door is closed
The work completed
It's best,
To step back
And …
Move away.

And– in your way.

Before

Where the house
Was before
The trees have come
Now.
Where the garden
Was before-
The flowers have
Come now.
And where ,
The house- garden
Was- is nearly
As the forest
Was before.
Seems all- we knew
Of before- has changed
To,
Now. From before.

Chiba

Twas on the way to Chiba
In far off Japan
Of years, nearly
Seventy or more ago
I can remember it plain- as seems
Part of a plan
A friend and I were
Told by a military member
Older than we to,
Wait on the veranda
Of a home, tell others
That came by –
And guide them on to Chiba
Nearby, with our jeep
The lady in the house
Was nice to my friend, and I
Gave us some tea, and o- sem- bi
On which to dine , as we waited,
To pass time by.
The day was nice- the weather too
Much time has passed, gone thru
Just where my friend
The others too, are now,
I'll never know
But this I know-
And will never forget
Twas on the way to Chiba
In far off Japan-
Of years- nearly
Seventy or more
Maybe so- of …
A long, long time-
Ago .

Things

Things can build and build
Till one can see or refuse, to see
That the pile can get – so very large
That it can fill, an auto garage
Till the auto will , have to stay-
Outside each day
For things have filled the garage
To stay. with things that build and build
And build and really have no right
To stay. A house can do this too
With things that stay-as they come thru.
Or any other place when one keeps
Too many things
They need not keep, as they-
Come thru…things pile, build.

See

You see the far away
I see more close
I see the far away too
You see oceans- I see ponds
I see oceans too
You see long streets
I see sidewalks
I see long streets too
You see wide open crystal sky
I see sky, some clouds too
I see wide open sky too.
I seen before, what …
You see too.

Rejoice

Got up today- went to church
Worshipped, with others at church
In an interesting worshipful way.
The church is a
Nice place to do that
The church of your choice on Sunday
Or any day of you desire
To get up , go there
Sometime – spend time-
In
Your way, and rejoice.

Song

The song was- stupendous
Inspiring,
It set a just
Wonderful
Pace.
The song was
Simply amazing
And was, lovely- Amazing Grace.

Its Way

Branches and leaves of green
I see on trees, trees seen-
Unseen too.
Move and sway of slight
Also in a way
That is smooth and lovely
Under skies of blue
Today with the wind,
That's here, but no one can-
See has never seen,
But lives and moves
It's special ways
In dark or light
Of day
And- branches and leaves
Of green
I see on trees- trees seen
Unseen too
Move and sway of slight,
Also in a way lovely-
Under skies of blue
Today
As the wind moves
Thru …
It's way.

Grows

Trimming- of trees, and shrubbery
Is a labor of work- that's quite great
Unless… to trim –as the great
Work of Creation does, not touched
Untouched – and, as of necessary
As it grows, with the beauty –
That it does. Trimming .

Much

Words are so lovely
And speak of so much- they speak of grief
Happiness, of the lovely,
With a love touch.
They start a war- bring about peace
With no words- much can be
With, without hostility, by action alone.
Ego loves words- inflames, good and bad.
Causing happiness, grief or sad
Words are so lovely – and speak so much.
Just how they are used
Spreads like sunshine
Leave's,
So much– words, words, words.

Cat Woman

The cat woman- the cat woman
Who lives with the cat woman,
Who lives with the cat woman ?
Nobody can live with the cat woman
For the cat woman, likes only cats
For the cat woman likes only cats
The cat woman- the cat woman
The cat woman,
Likes cats.

155

Music

Can you sing backward,
Now did you ever try ?
It might sound good
If you ever did-
It might sound good , real good
Also if lots of others – did too
Then we could hear
Backward , forward music,
When everybody was thru.
And that would be nice-
Maybe …Can you sing, backward ?

Friendly

Greedy , Greedy
Is easy to do
Easy to become that way
Driving happiness love
Far, far away.
But when friendly and love
Enter again – to stay
Greedy- greedy
Must , someway
Go away.

All Day

Nothing, nothing
My cat does nothing-she sleeps, she eats
Does nothing all day
Tho- she keeps, one eye slightly open-
And … keeps animals away
Cause ..
I've never seen an animal in my garage
Where she stays- like
An elephant, an alligator,
Or a Hippopotamus in my garage
She keeps them all away-
And does nothing else,
But sleeps all day, also …
Does her things- in a nice cats way.

Birthday

Today's a special day- least it is for me
Today's my wife's birthday
She's not here tho
The Creator called her about two years,
Ago, she left to stay
Today 15 September is her birthday
A special day for me
I'll remember it always
It's in my memory
Etched in my memory
We've been thru much together-
Almost 60 years of marriage together
Love builds, love builds
Understanding too comes becomes
The Creator builds it that way
Like stars , the moon, sunshine, that way.
Today's a special day
Least it is for me- its my wife's birthday
The Creator called her to stay
About two years ago- and …
Today would have been,
Her 90th birthday.

156

Memories

A friend passed on- had a funeral too
At the same church
My wife and I went to
My wife passed away-
About two years before,
Had her funeral too
At the same church before –with,
The same minister- the same funeral home
All too, in the same place
In front part of the church
Which must be,
Tho many memories came
Flooded my mind memories must be too,
For …
My wife and I spent
Fifty Eight lovely years together
And the memories were of
The thoughtful lovely kind
Passing thru my mind a silent way
At- our friends
Funeral service
Today .
And memories must be
They are healthful, also are
A large part of …
Humanity .

Faith

To have faith-faith in the mornings
Faith in the day- faith in the many ways
Each day comes to be.
For humanity, for the sun as
It has its run, thru the vast of sky
Then the healings, blessings-
That come from the Creator,
Coming secret lovely, to all.
To have faith- is a blessing
A spiritual eternal
Childlike lovely, given
To all creation
For the Creators- creation
And is beautiful- just beautiful
Faith given …
Made individually formed
Belived
Thru just …
And always,
Love.

Faith

To have faith.

Lost Moment

Work hard to make it thru
The lost moment-
The lost chance-
Might have helped.
You haven't got them- forget them,
You can make it thru without them.
Work hard – and …
You'll make it thru.

Late

When you go to bed late- and get up late
You miss, most of the day- passing thru
Because days have a special time
They must finish- when you get up late
You miss- most of the day
Passing thru,
The day , just … won't wait for you
If you , get up late.

Setting

The sun, right now
Is setting,
The sky of hue- is orange-ish blue
Evening hours are of long-
With dark appearing
Soon a sky of dark
Will be.
The sun right now
Is setting
Darkness silence-
And dark,
Very soon, will be.

Coming

Autumn's coming- in just a few days
Summer's almost gone
Soon Halloween, then Thanksgiving
Too, also winter and Christmas
Soon will come '
Then New Years, Valentine Day
Spring time- summer too
Autumn's coming
In just a few more days
Changing things slow,
Autumn's- special way.

A February Day

It's a February day
It's cold today
No birds in the sky
A crystal blue, clear sky
It's cold today
It's a February day
And there's sunshine too,
No birds are flying thru
It's cold today-
It's a February day.

Critters

Those little critters- like spiders, bugs
So small they be
They bite and move with quiet ease
But when the place they bite you
Later see- you'll remember
Those little critters cause …
You'll feel, you'll itch, you'll see,
You'll really see-
The place, they visited you-
You'll see.

Shining Over There

I can see a tiny little light shining
Far away-shining, shining thru the,
Window screen – look see it shining
Over there- shining, shining, almost
Most unseen, why it's shining
Over there no one I've seen ever knows-
Least none I've ever seen really
Tells me so.
Night's too that little light, late night-
Real late too- that little light- it
Just goes away.
If you look real , real, really close
Little feet nothing more- little hands
There too- no more, carry that light
Away, where they take that ljght
No one seems to know
They keep it far away, somewhere
Until the next night too, till 10;30
And plus two, then you can see
That light again shining far away
Shining thru the window screen
Over there, way over there almost
Most unseen—till …
Little feet , little hands, nothing more
No more
Keep it far away – take it …
Where no one I know
Seems to know
Till-until past 10;30
Plus two.
For few, and you, and me
To see. That tiny…light

Shining .

Came

It didn't come- on
Any day of the week,
Like-
A Monday, Tuesday , Wednesday ,
Thursday, Friday, a Saturday, or Sunday.
It didn't come on ,
Any season of the year
Like-
Spring, summer, autumn,
Or winter.
It came – right after
The old and the
New of the year
Way … out on the
Outskirts of time.
That's-
When it came, that thing.
That's …
When it came,
And nobody seen it-
Don't know what it was.

Gotta Do

You have to do- what you gotta do
So quit griping, and do it
Quit griping – hear …
And do it , learn to like it
Even if you hate it
Ya gotta do it- so shut up-
Gosh … you have to do ,
What you gotta do
And that's it.

Was

It was day, time had passed too,
It was morning, noon time
Afternoon too-
Twilight evening
Night time too
It was still that day- but …
It – had most,
Passed … thru.

Blessed

I am blessed- we can say
Without conviction when we say
In the blessings we receive
From the Creator, each day.
I am blessed is something
Beautiful for each to think and say
I am blessed, I am blessed
When blessed … One can feel,
By the Creator- each day.
For – then,
I truly, very truly – am blessed.

Dreams

In dreams, what the mind
Sees and feels and makes- that's
What the brain comprehends
Sees and feels and makes
One can almost sometime, depending
On what and how late one eats,
Time to time, one can really almost
Think and see some real weird things and
Nearly be almost halfway or near awake.
That's mostly when the weird to be
One can and some remember to
Actually see,
Dreams are strange, sometime
Just really strange.

Fair

Keep your distance- keep your distance
Keep your distance, that's-
The thing to do- keep your distance
Stay away- best you really do,
Don't mix with em- if you do, keep it
Of fair play- that's the only way,
Keep your distance- keep your distance
Keep it … by fair play.

Knows

Who knows which way the wind
For sure will blow, and…
The exact time, who knows for sure
How long a war will last when
A war is begun-who knows for sure
Which way and how far any bird will fly
Who knows-which star next, will fall
The Creator of course, anyone else …
You know … who knows.

I Think

Today- I think maybe
I ruined today
I started it off in the wrong, wrong
Way
I stayed up too late
Till the start of day
That's the wrong way-
To start a day
I know that,
I try to stop it too
But still most times I do
Stay up too late
Till the start of day
Since my spouse has left, to stay
Been called away, I've mostly done
That way,
I've got to stop that tho
I know that too- I just right now
Find it hard , very hard to do, today too-
I think maybe I ruined today
I started it off , in the wrong way-
When I stayed up too late
Lost most of today again, that way.

Sleep

Set my alarm and went to sleep
And thought I heard to hear in my house.
People walking all around talking
Closing doors, walking ,running
Outside too, very active doing things
That people do.
I awakened quick to check on all that
I did hear, and found my alarm
Still on all was quite ok,
It must have been a dreamy dream.
Twas all that I did hear
Dreams have a way- they do,
Passing thru. During sleep.

Body

Sleep rest the body must have
Sleep rest give the body
It's sleep rest
The body will usually
Do the rest
If possible
But it must have
It's
Sleep rest.

End Start

At end of day- put the sun away
Turn off twilight
Bring out evening
Starlight, moonlight
Deep blue dark, of night
Till dawn, mornings
Light of day
And … then
Start another day.

To Me

I see, a shadow with wings
Moving on the ground
Maybe it came, from a bird-
Close around flying not too high
In the sky … cause,
The shadow moved fast
On the ground with wings.
The shadow I did see
Twas surely from a bird,
Least seemed so … to me

Secrets

Every house has secrets
It keeps within its walls
They're quiet and few
They know
Those few are hardly spoken
About,
At all
But they know those secrets of,
Very, very few
Tho– and,
The house speaks its way
Sometime
With squeaks
Doors opening closing
Windows odors, noises
Sounds too
Spooky, ghostly, acceptable
The house, the house knows too but,
Every house has secrets
It keeps within its walls
Hardly speaks about it
At all, only...sometime.

Heard

I just heard it- on the radio
I did, I did, I really did
That the modified, death on wheels
The super worm's are- on their way
Will be hard to stop
Until they drop- will maybe be
Where there is corn
I heard it on the radio, in early morn
I did, I did, I really did
I just heard it
Oh my, oh me-
Oh me, oh my.

Camping

I plan to go camping
Where the wild and quiet are free,
Where the deer and the bear-
And rabbits, squirrels are …
Where birds fly chatter
Hawks fly too, also crows
Many crows fly here- there
See everything
The way crows do,
Mountain lions may walk.
Sometime sea gulls fly too,
I plan to go camping
Where the wild
And quiet are free,
Come-
Go camping,
With me.

Style

Live a style for a long, long while
One likes that style,
To change that style
Is hard to do, and stay till thru
For that style, becomes slow, slow
Your style, you live-that style
You maybe ,like that style-that is …
In secret-secretly
Your , style...for-

A, long, long while.

Tonight

We ate out together tonight
We had a good time together too
To eat out together
Have a good time together
Is a good thing for any family
Sometime to do.
We did …
We ate out together, tonight.

Quiet

After the family has grown up and gone
The house with two, moves slow along
Till after one or other
Of the two has left
Is called away to stay
The house inside out too
Almost- like , almost – then
Never moves
Is …
Real quiet
Tho,
Not thru, for-
Shadows rich memories of past
Stay there, felt …
Too –
After, after
In the after,
Passing thru.

Will Do

A pickup, a pickup, a pickup,
A pickup
A small truck-
With four wheels and a box
To move small things
Not too far-but enough.
To not have a pickup
Now that's ok too
For a car, not a horse
Not an elephant- not a goat
But a car
A car will do
Keep the pickup- tho,
Keep the pickup, the pickup,
The pickup … For with,
It's box and it's four wheels-
It will do.

Away

I went away
To look for the world
And the world went
To look for me
We met halfway
And our homes
Were far away
Oh dearie me
I went away-and the world
Stayed with me
Oh dearie me
Now the world, I see-
It's all around me.

Toy

A child can take, most anything- safe,
And make a toy- to play
Then play, and play
Much time away.
For the child, enjoys that toy
Because, that toy is
A real, very real
Child's toy, and picked
By the child.

Tree Branches

I see tree branches
With leaves of green
Gently waving
Waving, waving, waving,
With the wind
Against the blue of sky.
As the wind blows
Ever softly, by.
They are beautiful, lovely too
Waving, waving, waving,
With the wind-
As the wind blows thru … Today-
I see tree branches
With leaves of green
Waving, waving,waving,
Softly, gently,
Their way
In the wind.

A Restaurant

It's nice to eat
At a restaurant sometime – tho
You eat rather quickly and pay
Then you leave
When you do .
It's just nice to eat out
In a restaurant sometime
Where the food is the same
But not quite the same
As the food at home too
It's nice to eat
At a restaurant-
It's nice to eat out
It's just nice …
To eat out- sometime,
Too .

Beautiful

Say , how are you today ?
I really miss being near you
You are so beautiful
Lovely too
I think about the times
We've spent together
I love being near you
You are the most lovely
Beach near the ocean,
In this area -
Say ,
How are you today ?

Is It

To agree to not disagree
Or to,
Not disagree
To agree
Is almost- the same
But not really
The same
Disagreement
Or is it
Really to agree
Really ,really
Now – don't disagree … Tho
Is it ? Really.

Clyde

River Clyde- River Clyde
Way over in Scotland
Is River Clyde
And so much changed is
River Clyde
At low tide, it seems that one could
Swim or walk
To the other side
But so very ,very deep
Is
The River Clyde
That ships can travel
On River Clyde, at low tide
Be careful, careful
On River Clyde
Way over in Scotland
Is ,
The River Clyde.

The Morning

The sun in the morning
It brightens the day
And when you're together
Or alone- especially,
It brightens both inside
And outside
In beautiful ways-
The sun in the morning
Oh, the beautiful
Sun …
In the morning.

Left

A tree, a tree- is a living ..
Something of beauty
Just to see-and
When it was planted in memory
Of one who left for another
Place forever to be
Those here with memories
Thru love, will remember
The one who left, for forever,
That very special one thru
Memories and that tree- a tree
A little living oriental maple tree.
Is something of beauty
Just to see especially … for me,
For it was planted in memory
Of a loved one,
My wife, who left-
For forever, to be.

Contribution

Some written, or recorded- info.
In some way
Of what one- did see or feel,
While passing thru
For others to see- is,
A small contribution
To humanity.
And contributions
Written or recorded
In some way- helps …
Construct History –
Family, history,
Too .

Sounds

Sing like the wind blows
Just any old way- and when the
Sounds come out, they sound good
Tho … but- just any old way,
And – that's ok. Just sing.

Gone

The past is gone
Like notes of a song
As stars, of yesterday's night
Past by,
Out of sight.
Let it go –
Forget it, move on to new
Twill make
Of new- you …
The past is gone
Forget it.

The Best Way

Forgive, forgive, forgive
It gives an inner joy
It gives a brand new start-it brings
Joy to the heart.
And brings a love all can enjoy,
Forgive, forgive, forgive
Each day.
That is – the best
Creation's way,
To … forgive.

Where's David

Where's David ?
Where's David ?
David's our Teddy Bear
Oh- she's got David
She's got David
David our,
" Teddy " Bear,
Yes … She's got David
Give me David, " Right Now "
No way
" Remember "
You gotta share
Ok – maybe …
Later
Ok .

Animal Suits

There's a tiger walking around
On two feet, and an alligator too
Oh, I see a dog that's watching them
While they are walking thru.
But the alligator tiger and the dog
Yes, the dog is too,
Only children in animal suits
They're wearing.
Walking everywhere,
From here to there
All over the place,
While they play right here-
Walking around
Having fun in animal suits,
With everyone

Yellow Round Moon

I watched the full yellow
Round moon
Rise in a partially cloud filled sky
High slow and up thru clouds
To it's place in the sky
As it's done and will do
While the Earth passes thru
Watching the full yellow
Round Moon rise in the sky
Is an interesting something to do
Sometime …
Try it too.

For Free

When gone so low one cannot
More go
And must look up to see
The sky above- that offer's free
So much with love that there
Will always be plenty, everywhere-
Just to look, and- just to see, so wonderful-
Feels so very wonderful to look
Up and see- yes … Finally, the sky
So free be it day or night
Or when ere it be. When gone so low
One cannot more go, and must
Look up to see the sky above
That offer's love when ere- where ere
We be, it's there and all … for free
It's wonderful- it's wonderful
When low, to look up
And see- the comfort of the sky.

Carry

Child, teen, adult something comes
It unseen stays, light heavy too
On our shoulders, stays
Thru nights, thru days- thru years
On shoulders lays
Our shoulders know
It stays there tho
And they may move slight forward too
Our face may show small wrinkles too
As with the years we move
Slow rapid thru, all from this
Something unseen on our shoulders
That's become our load in life-
Few know of as we, quiet it we carry
Differently , quietly, our load,
Our personal load …
Our life, thru. All must do.

Size

I looked at the moon
In the sky tonight
To determine the size of the moon
And found that the moon
Was of half size
That lit the world tonight
Among the few clouds
That were in the sky
And the sky was blue
Dark blue was the sky
While the half moon, quite beautiful
Lit the sky
As I looked at the moon
In the sky tonight
To determine
The size- of the moon.

Of Day

The day- the night
The morning too, and in between
The day- the night
Comes evening, then night
And after that,
The light of day

Came

The rains- the rains
The most, most storms
Of rains came down
And after the storm, a rainbow
Came , a beautiful rainbow
Came, too- after ... the rains,
And storms- came thru.

Calling

I hear the birds
I hear the birds
I hear the birds calling
Listen, listen
Oh listen
The haunting call
Of the pigeon birds
I heard the birds
I heard the birds
Did you hear the birds?
The birds
The birds they
Were calling they
Were calling, calling
Calling, calling
Calling
The birds were calling
Did you hear the birds?
The haunting call...of-
The pigeon, bird...The birds,
The birds, those birds

The Sun

Oh how lovely, beautiful
It is to see
The flowers, the trees, the grass,
The leaves, and all the beautiful
Lovely- that only
The sun can do ... will do,
Oh how lovely beautiful
The Sun.

To You

It's a lovely morning
The sky is blue
The sun is shining
The moon is there too
Real faint in the sky
Waiting for dark to come by
And how are you , as
This morning passes thru
It's a lovely morning,
Good morning-
To you.

Smart

The plants and animals
How smart they be
The way they've grown as we
To be as smart – or maybe
Smarter than we-
If …
Plants need water- we water them
Plants need pollen- we give them bees
Plants need fertilizer- we give them the best
Animals too …
Animals need food water- we supply, we give
Animals need shelter- we supply, we give
Animals need love- we supply, we give
The plants and animals- now, we be- as
Maybe they, want us to be
How smart they be
The way they've grown- as we
To be as smart – or maybe
Smarter than we-
For …
We must perform- their desires tor
The friends … they be
Of course- they…
Most are for food, too
Nothings – free.

Same

The morning looks almost
The same as noon in the sky
But the sun has moved
A little- to let, the morning go by
And let the noon in,
When morning was nigh
The morning and noon
Are good friends in the sky
The afternoon tho-
Seems to be more like,
Evening twilight and noon
Then, wait's for the day
To pass by. But…

The morning looks almost

As noon in the sky.

The Lady

The lady I met
That stayed with me for years
Of nearly sixty
She was a- special lady
That stayed with me
She was my wife
She left about
Two years ago
But has a special place
In my memory
The lady I met
My wife.

Bothers

Whatever bothers
The situation
Most
Will most
Perhaps …
Reveal the truth-
Of the situation,
Most.

Spring

It's February now
It's almost Spring
The days are getting longer
A little more sunny too
Trees will blossom
When Spring comes thru
With the blossoms
As they come
Then the flowers
As they do
Will show us in a way
The power of a love
Just imagine …
It's February-
Why,
It's almost- Spring.

Quietly

The quiet of quiet
We cannot see
It creeps so very quietly
And then if a noise appears
It soon disappears, quite quietly
Quiet soon returns as-
The quiet of quiet
We cannot see
Felt, oh so very-
Quietly

Speak Silently

Tho you're not here
Since you left- to see
You're here in a way
To me
You speak silently
In a way
I can hear- I perhaps, only
Quietly, silently
Like a soft breeze
Seen by the one- it's
Composed for seemingly to see
Missed by others, perhaps-
Entirely ,
Tho you're not here
Since you left- to see
You're here in a way
To me,
You speak, silently.

The World

The world contains
Many, many things
We know so much about
The world contains
Many, many things
We know very little about
And the world moves on each day
In it's own constant
Seemingly rate and way
And we are amazed
As we move on our way
While the world survives moving
Constantly at it's
Seemingly constant
Rate containing many
Many things, we know
Very little, and much about.

I Wonder

I sometime wonder
If those we see- in old
Pictures we have, we find in books
Somewhere put away- long ago,
I wonder just … what,
They would say- if we …
Spoke with them today.
Would they say Hi,
How are you, where have
You been, Or …
Would they speak of the
Where or time the picture
Was taken in.
I sometime wonder, just …
What those- in our books
Of old pictures would say,
If we spoke to them today.
What do you think they
Would say ?

Sunday Morning

It's Sunday morning
Most everything's closed
Folks wearing nice clothes
Folks sleeping late
Some travelin too
Some fightin
Some doin good
It's Sunday morning
Monday's coming too.

Beauty

Hazy the hills, of far away
Green the hills, of close
The blue of sky
And the sunlight too.
Bring beauty of the two
Just oh,
So softly,
Thru.

Unfold

To just unfold- like,
A book, the seasons, a flower
A storm- a rainbow
A child, thru to adult
Or anything … unfold, open,
Come alive-
Is a beautiful, a wonderful
Difficult thing to do.
And it's marvelous simply lovely
Trying and marvelous to see
All the way thru.
Something, someone, somebody
Just to unfold, blossom out
Become and achieve
Their hearts desire
Thru unfolding thru
Life's many paths, steps
And things, people …
Must meander-trudging,
Growing on the way.

This Morning

The birds are twittering
This morning
They're singing soft loud
Twittering thru
And their music, makes morning
More nice, in it's way
The birds are twittering
This morning,
This day.

Wonderfully

The sky is clear
No clouds- in the sky
The sky is- all over blue
It makes a,
Most beautiful day, with the-
Sunshine, just … simply, wonderfully
Beautiful, shining- thru.

The Place

I want to see the place
The place where
I first met you
Then twill be almost as new-
The place where first I met you
Tho new, the place is near
Ten thousand miles away,
In another land, it can be done
I'm sure it can
I want to see the place
Where I first met you
Tho it is far away
And you have been called
Away to stay.
I want to see the place
Where I first met you
Then it again will be, as today.

Write

I write of past
It comes to me
Of years, years past
I then
Can think, and see.
My pen perhaps
Thru me,
Has memory.
Beautifully
When I write of past,
It comes to me.

Gone Away

This part of the park
Is quiet- today
All have gone away
If it stay's that way all day,
Or if it stay's for awhile
That way.
Maybe, I will
Complete this story
I am writing –
Today.

Daylight

The Daylight leaves slow
Like it don't want to go
And dark pushes it away
Then night comes-
Dark and night are friends,
They stay- then, till daylight
Comes again.
The daylight
Tho,
Leaves slow.

The Mountains

I look to the mountains
Where green there doth lie
I look to the mountains
Solemn quiet there
Seems to lie
I look to the mountains
See a Hawk soar
The sky
I look to the mountains
Unknown there
Doth lie
I look to the mountains
I look at the mountains
Today-
In the far, far away
Where the forever
Doth stay-
In the mountains,
The mountains.

Similar

The ending the ending
Is so near the beginning
That the ending and
The beginning they are
Almost as one
And to be as one
Each must have much
The same as the other one
So beginnings and endings
Perhaps in many ways
Like
Night time and day time
Cast light at sometime
In much the very same way
The endings beginnings if one checks close
Have much very similar
In many of similar
Ways thus
Keeping life interesting
Daily in similar ways.

Singing

It's night time
The frogs are singing
Their songs
Of the evening,
Their songs
Of the night.
It's night time
The frogs
Are singing,
Tonight.

A Certain

Where the mountains
And the waters
And the hilltops
Meet the sky
Therein
A certain silent
Beauty,
Doth lie.

Night

It's clear
It's cool
It's evening
With little light-
It's almost night.
It will be,
Maybe-
A beautiful ,
Night.

Sailing By

I seen a Hawk go sailing by
With wings outstretched
I seen him fly
Not once his wings
I seen him flap
And in seconds, so very fast
He did sail- from me,
For him to see-
Then see him not.
I did not know- a Hawk
Could sail
In sky- so fast
As that.

A Little Lizard

I seen a little lizaard
It stopped and looked at me
And then- it thought, perhaps-
That thing is so big,
And from the way it stares at me
It just might spoil my day.
I best, must … leave this person
Thing, and, be on my way
The little lizard- quickly left.

Seems

Tonight,
The branches and green leaves
Of trees- are… near still,
Against faint blue
Of sky
The wind seems faint
On high
The trees of tall,
Move slight
Of now- near fall
Of night
To night.
The wind seems faint
On high
Against faint blue
Of sky.

Mountainous

The mountains
I see
Surrounding me
They're beautiful
Hazy and-
Far away
Also- seem so serenely
Quiet too.
Emitting that,
Serene quiet-
Beautiful, everywhere
Over here
Very lovely, lovely view.
Of …
Just mountainous
Surrounding's,
Too.

Doing Nothing

Doing nothing, doing nothing
It's not good to be- constantly
Doing nothing.
Because if doing nothing
Is all you do … soon
Doing nothing,
Will do away …
With   you.

Tonight

I rode my bicycle
In the moonlight tonight
Under the round yellow moon
In the moonlit sky
And what I remember
Of sounds I could hear
Are sounds of the wind
Whistling by in my ears
As I went thru the air
And the song of the bicycle
Tires humming on the street
As I rolled along while
I rode my bicycle
Under the round yellow moon
In the moonlight tonight.

I Seen

This afternoon, I seen the sun
Right up in the sky, all round
And yellow and way up high
The clouds were drifting
To cover the sun
But the sun shined thru
This I seen- the sun it do.
This afternoon, when I seen
The sun right up in the sky
All round, and yellow- and,
Way…
Up in the sky.

Two Seats

On …
The tricycle
With two seats
Two can ride
Two can talk
Two can have more
Fun than one
The tricycle with
Two seats
Is- neat.

A Bicycle

Ride a bicycle as you go
You can sit down and walk
Sing songs, hum, whistle, think-
Talk too, ride a bicycle- as you go
That's a really nice way to go
As you go – on your way by …
Riding a bicycle
Thru.

Finished

When something's finished- it's over
Except for the memories
They're yours to keep
The experience too
Earned by the something
You went thru
There's a time and a place
For everything
Taught by Creation, when Creation
Was created never to be forgotten
As life unfolds- with love in it's
Many ways, when something's over
It's finished move on
With memories, from that day.
Told in and with love.

A Way Thru

There's a way thru the dark
There's a way- there's a way
Tho it seems all is lost- all is lost
There's a way, tho you've lost all
It seems-that you've prized.
Is lost too- there's a way
For as the sun shines by day
Also moon stars at night rainbows
Too after storms, they light
The sky above with love
The
Creators love spiritually, lovely,
Eternally beautifully
There's a way-which will be
Given in due time
A time and place exists
For everything believe with
Faith and remember
Always remember
Memories are from a special
Love too, there's a way-
Thru the dark … there's a way
Thru.

In The Sky

For a quarter moon
There's always room in the sky
To watch darkness
As it floats soft
All over below, and yet high
In a night time sky
While lights in a
Valley far below
Glow with bright
Thru the dark, down low
At the quarter moon
Where there's always room
In it's space, soft … yet high
In a night, time sky.

Everyday

Mistakes, mistakes
Why they're easy to do
I make em everyday
Most everybody does
And you make em your way
Mostly in what you do
And what you say
But you just gotta say,
Excuse me in your way
And do what you gotta do
That's honest and good to do
Till you're thru
The best you know how to do
Don't worry much, cause,
Everybody I know has mistakes,
Mistakes, they make em everyday
Nobody's perfect, least that way.

They Hide

Shadows they hide, in the dark
Those guys
They see you , as you
Walk by – those guys-
They hide in the dark
Cause they like the dark
And if you have, a light
That can shine in the dark
And your shadow you see
Listen close,
And you might hear
Your shadow laugh and say,
Hee, hee, hee,
Cause shadows they see
And they-
Hide in the dark
Cause- they, those shadows-
Those Guys,
They … like the dark.

Perfect Way

A ride in a-
Hot air balloon
Swinging in a basket
Fresh air all around,
Seems to me-
Twould be great
Just…
To soar thru the air
At,
The speed of wind, rate.
And watch the country side
Float,-just-slow, by-
Seems to me
On a clear sky
Blue day.
A ride in the basket
Swinging below a
Hot air balloon
Watching the country side
Float slow-by.
Would be a near perfect way
To quiet slow
With the wind-
Fly by.

Roof

I see birds-running,
Walking down the roof
And the roof is high
The birds can't fall
And the birds don't care-
Cause the birds
Can fly.

Childhood

Its fun to do
What as a child
We've done
Something's we do
All life time thru.
For in each one
A child's life stays
That is awakened
By what we do
In some way
On
Some days
Those things
We've done
During…
Childhood days.
Oh, its fun to do-great fun to do,
Something's
What as a child
We've done,
Sometime-
All-
Lifetime, thru.

Halfmoon

Moonlight moonlight
Halfmoon too
You light the world
With soft
Mysterious light,
Sunlights thru.
Its
Just lovely-
Tonight.

Each Day

It's new
Each day
Seems planned
That way
Or what we do
We do our way.
The things we do
Along the way
Along the road
Of life.

It's new
They're new
Each day.

Me

Come talk to me
Come talk with me
Tonight
Let's talk of all
What is to be
Let's talk of all
That used to be
Let's talk of what
That just might be
Come talk to me
Come talk with me
You were that be
You could not be
You are to be
That could not be
But are to me
I think as me
Come talk to me
Come talk with me,
Be me…
Tonight.

Sun Setting

In the evening
Near sun setting time
Shadows getting longer
Longer shadow lines.
With a sky of-
Crystal blue
Mid dropping sun
Near sunset too.
Tis time of quiet
And lovely-lovely
Slips thru.
In the evening-
Near sun setting
Time.

Dress

The pink dress
With flowers
The lady wore
Was beautiful-
Silent beauty,
Flowed thru.
As she walked
In the pink
Dress
With flowers
Her way, that day

Wind

About the wind
About the wind
About the wind
What's so nice
About the wind?
Sometimes it changes
Does the wind
And sometimes…
Let's you win-does the wind
About the wind-about the wind
About the wind
That's so nice
About the wind-about the wind
About the wind
At times-
Sometimes…that's nice.

Together

Across the Stretches
Of life…
No matter
The valley's, hills,
Mountains, plains
Strife there maybe.
Losses, gains
Whatever,
As long as-
Communication
Love, honest love,
Family love
Creations love-
Remain.
Across the stretches
Tho there be
Of wretched.
Love-Love
Binds...together
All.
For true loves,
Free.

Songs

There's A Reason

Arr. by GIANNI STAIANO

AL VICENT

Slow Gospel swing

I.

There's a

rea - son for the sun - shine in the sky   There's a
rea - son that God sends his love each day   To each

rea - son why the birds fly by on high   For this is
one in his own ve - ry spe-cial way   For this is

love in Na-ture's way for love al - ways finds a way There's a
love from God a-bove and God's love it finds a way

185

187

Excuse Me

AL VICENT

bless-ings and min-gle with us   Ex-cuse me please but did you

see him___ pass this way to-day?   oh if he

passed   did he leave   a mes-sage   Was there a

190

sign that he might pass this way a - gain Did he

stop heal the sick and help the low - ly? Ex-cuse me

please but did you see Je sus____ pass this way to- day?

None passed this way except the stran-ger who said, Come let the lit-tle

chil-dren sit on my knee. But they said the stran ger's arms were open

wide and from somewhere deep down in - side That love just flowed and in it's

192

stran - ger   was   Je - sus   Ex-cuse me please   may-be the

stran - ger   was   Je - sus   Who passed this

way   who passed this   way

A Flag

AL VICENT

A flag for you a flag for me a flag for e - very-one that's

free A flag of red and white and blue___ that means that oth-ers thought of you

___ And lived and loved and died for you___ A flag for you a flag for

me a flag for ev-ery-one that's free___ our flag of red and white and blue

___ A flag of love for me and you___

Christmas Tree

AL VICENT

2

In a man-ger far a-way, In the ci-ty of Beth-le-hem,
Near the man-ger far a-way, o'er the ci-ty of Beth-le-hem,

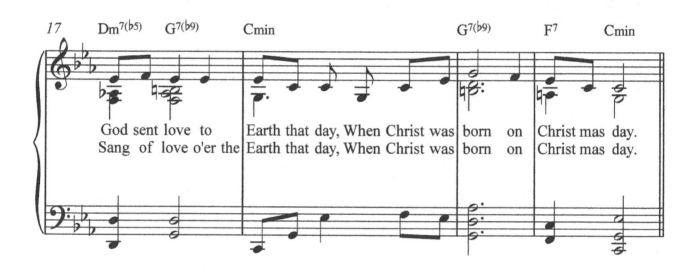

God sent love to Earth that day, When Christ was born on Christ mas day.
Sang of love o'er the Earth that day, When Christ was born on Christ mas day.

Shep-herds came on Christ-mas day, To the man-ger far a-way,
Peace on Earth on Christ-mas day, from a man-ger far a-way,

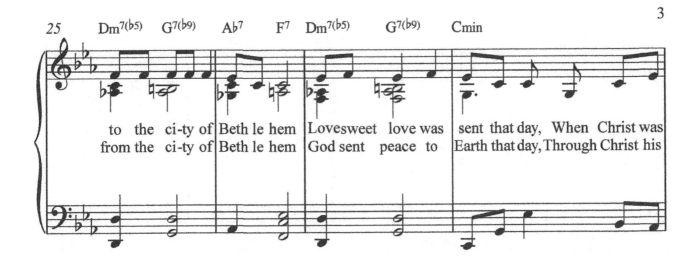

4

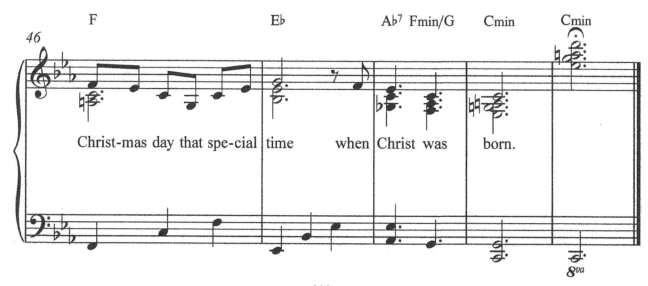

Stories

Tree House

The Tree was small and as it grew, in the country other grew near it, animals came sometimes. Then children found the nice the nice open spot because a small road was close by where people with old cars and horses pulling wagons, and oxen too pulling wagons. Oxen were different but very very strong. They could pull very big loads most of the time. The oxen and horses pulling wagons would come by making tracks leaving marks on the ground. Then old cars would go where the wagons went along and soon there was a road. The tracks got deeper and deeper as the years went by making a pretty good little road. The horses and wagons went other places too, other roads were made and only people that had to go by where the tree was growing went near the place was.

The trees though kept growing. There was an open space near the tree where animals could come stay and lay down. Soon children too would come play close by the little tree and the tree grew and grew. One day as the tree got taller and taller, children started to climb the tree. As the tree grew, the limbs grew long and strong from the trunk of the tree and the tree grew leaves that give a nice shade under it.

More animals came to lay there, more children to play there because it was cool there in the shade from the hot summer sun. A little girl climbed the tree and found the limbs were pretty strong and decided to get her books and climb the tree, sit there and read in the shade where it was usually quiet.

Little boys had different ideas, they liked very such to climb the tree too. They decided after much discussion among them that up about 15 feet above the ground where the tree branched out to kind of a "Y" shape, that maybe some boards could be put there to sit on and when the wind blew the tree it would be like a ship in the water. Or maybe even a pirate ship sailing over the ocean to places off far, far, far, away. The boys thought that over a few days; it was a big decision. How to keep the material up there and safe in a tree, especially about 15 feet above the ground. That's a long way to fall out of a moving tree.

The boys altogether decided it would be a good idea to make the platform. The country town was very small there were only about 3 or 4 boys. The only problem they could think of was where would they get enough strong boards and get them up there and put the platform together in the tree. The boys started looking everywhere for the boards and material around their houses, just anywhere. Finding boards is not an easy to do project like the boys were undertaking making a pirate ship platform in a tree. The more the boys looked the more desirable the project became and imaginations of pirate ships sailing on oceans to far away places like china or other places far far away with large treasure chests.

As the boys would find material they decided a good place to keep it where it would be safe. They found some bushes not far from the tree kind of far back under the bushes so it would be hard to see. The place was alright, no one bothered the material the boys gathered as it could be found when they finally got enough material to start the platform. They found it was not easy to make a platform for a tree and get it that high. Then make it stay there so it could be used as a pirate ship. Some boys wanted it to be an airplane too but that was ok everybody worked hard. Their parents always knew where they were, even the little girl who read her book in the tree would come sit and watch as she was comfortable reading the boys working on the platform and asked, "What are you doing?" The boys would tell her it's a secret.

Finally the platform was finished. It took a long time, many smashed fingers form nails that bent from young boy carpenter hammer strokes. But a finished product, the boys were proud of. The only problem the boys had now was how to get the platform up nearly 15 feet and fasten it in the tree and still be in one piece. Nobody thought about it before but it now was a problem. It was too heavy for the boys to lift. They did not want to ask many others because it was their secret project. After much pondering on the now complete platform it was decided to dismantle the project and reassemble it piece by piece in the tree and on strong branches tie securely. It took quite a long time and a lot of work but finally the platform was complete. The boys had a little kool aid and cookie party and a lot of fun playing on their pirate ship tree platform with summer wind rustling the tree leaves.

Later it was decided to gather more material and makes sides and a top on the platform and finally a door. The project then became a little tree house where very much fun was experienced climbing up and down the ladder. The boys even let the little girl read her books there sometimes when they weren't using the tree house. She used it a few times but not too much because she liked an open tree where she could feel the open free blowing breeze with nor so many boy things around. So she found another place.

I think maybe it was in a tree too but the boys had many hours of fun from the tree house they made in the little tree that grew in the nice open spot in the country with a small road close by where horses and oxen pulling wagons. Later old cars passed by and an old steam choo choo train blowing its whistle ringing its bell too sometime passed trough. The little tree grew and the boys and the girl grew. I remember too that little tree where we all had fun way out in the country under the wide open sky in the country sun. For I was one of those boys, and the little girl was my sister the others my friends. In that little Michigan town from years many past, of a long, long, time ago.

Gertrude and Heathcliff

"Gertrude lets stop here, we've come a long way all the way from Florida. I'm tired. You must be too."

"Ok Heathcliff," said Gertrude "This looks like a nice place."

"It is, I've seen it before when we were near here. I think people call this place Wisconsin Gertrude. I think this might be a nice place to stay all summer too. We can fly all over and see lots of things. Not too many of our friends are here though."

"We can rest here tonight. I saw a little stream over there Heathcliff. Im sure we can find some plants, insects, or food we like. This looks like a nice place."

"It is, It looks nice."

Gertrude and Heathcliff are Sand Hill Cranes. They like to wade in the water, have long legs for doing so, and are also quite skillful catching fish things edible for them in water. The next day Heathcliff and Gertrude flew several places, met some friends they knew but not many. Sometimes they would fly a nice place with a fresh water stream and stay there for several days. There was always lots of good things Gertrude and Heathcliff could find to eat near freshwater.

One day Heathcliff and Gertrude were preening their feathers with mud near the stream. They liked to do this when a turtle walked by. "That looks like the same turtle I saw a long time ago maybe four of five seasons ago when we came here isn't It Gertrude?" asked Heathcliff.

"Yes it looks like the same turtle." Said Gertrude

"I'm going to ask that turtle where he is going and what he does here."

"That's not your business Heathcliff. Leave the turtle alone. Besides you don't understand what turtles say."

"Maybe I might. I'm going to try."

"How are you going to talk to the turtle Heathcliff?"

"I don't know Gertrude. I could stand in from of him."

"You better not Heathcliff. I understand turtle bite hard, he might bite your foot. You know we have to wade in water for food like fish and things we like."

"Yes that's right. Let me think, I could walk close to him maybe he would look up and see me and I could talk to him?"

"That would not be a good idea either Heathcliff." Said Gertrude, "He might look up and see you and stop, go back in his shell. You are so much taller than the turtle."

"Maybe you are right Gertrude, maybe you are right. I would still like to talk to the turtle the next time I see it. I want to talk to him."

"You better hurry Heathcliff because the season is getting short here, We must leave soon."

"I know, I know Gertrude. I'll think of something. But I was thinking the other day and I thought maybe I should ask for help how to do what I need to do. Maybe I'll ask a crow. Crow's are everywhere and they see everything."

"You cant talk to crows."

"But I can send the crow a bird message. He's another bird. Tomorrow I'll try."

"This should be interesting." Said Gertrude.

The next day at the stream Heathcliff tried to send his message several times but nothing happened. Then suddenly two crows very near Gertrude and Heathcliff sending a universal bird message.

"We received your message. We are special messengers we usually don't talk to cranes but this is special. Is everything alright? How can we crows help?"

"Thank you for answering" Heathcliff answered "We are alright. I just wanted to know how best to converse with a turtle?"

"A turtle? Why would you want to talk to a turtle?"

"No special reason I just wanted to."

"We don't know we'll be back it might take some time. Mr. Owl might be sleeping. Mr. Woodpecker we can usually hear him. He's always knocking on something. We'll be back."

"We'll be here" said Heathcliff and Gertrude, "Thank you."

"That's ok" said the crows "It's nice to have something new to do. No one has ever asked we special messengers to do anything before."

So Gertrude and Heathcliff waited and waited and waited. They saw something climg slow.

"Gertrude" said Heathcliff. "That's the turtle. He must be going home."

"Yes" said Gertrude "it's almost dark. Heathcliff I'm going to stand in front of him and see what he does."

"You better not Heathcliff its near sleep time he might not like it."

"I'll be careful. I'll keep far away."

Heathcliff stepped in front of the turtle. The turtle stopped looked up at heathcliff and went back in his shell, stayed for awhile and then came out again. It looked around and went home. The next morning the messenger crows came back. They said Mr. Owl and Mr. Woodpecker both said to knock on the turtle shell. Some turtles understand bird messages but yo might have to get a mallard duck to interpret to the turtles talk to mallard ducks and bullfrog sometimes. The crows said they knew a mallard duck and a bullfrog if necessary they could ask to come by if needed send us a bird message.

"Ok and thank you." Said the messenger crows. "Call us anytime, we know you now." And they flew away together.

Heathciff and Gertrude together said "That was interesting."

The next day Heathcliff and Gerrude watched looking for the turtle. About noontime the turtle came slowly walking by. Heathcliff and Gertrude watched then Heatchliff told Gertrude "I think I'll just go tap him with my bill on his shell, I'll walk behind him and tap."

"Ok. I'll stand here and watch." Said Gertrude.

Heathcliff walked hehind the turtle bent over tapped on the turtles shell. The turtle stopped and went back in his shell, stayed there awhile then started walking again. Heathcliff tapped again. The turtle went in his shell again. About that time the crows came and then a mallard duck came landed close to Heathcliff and Gertrude. Then quite a large bullfrog came and a snake and a mouse.

The crows said "We told our friends the mallard duck and bullfrog what you wanted to do. They told their friends the snake and the mouse they are special messengers in their families too and they wanted to come also. We thought the turtle might walk by so lets get started. Ou start Mr. Crane."

Heathcliff said "I tapped the shell two times already the turtle went back inside both times. Maybe he will come out soon again."

Everyone waited and soon the turtle came out and started walking. Heathcliff tapped the shell again the turtle must have been annoyed with sso much tapping on his shell. The turtle stopped and stretched his neck, turned his head around and looked to see everyone. Then Heatcliff sent a bird message after bending down low close to the turtle saying "Hello, hello I'm Heathcliff with my friends. We want to say hello, how are you. Everybody else here are my friends."

The turtle turned around for a better look then sent messages back. "I'm fine , I'm fine."

Heathcliff was happy, "You understand me."

"Yes" said the turtle, "I understand you." Then the mallard duck, the bullfrog, the mouse, and the snake all sent messages to the turtle. Everyone had a very good time sending messages everyone understood. Heathcliff found out the turtle went everyday to see his friends other turtles living not too far away. Others who lived very far away sometimes it would take a few days to get to see time so he would just stop in a safe place and go inside his shell to sleep, wake up and keep going till he got there. Then he would come back or if the place was better just move there. The crows all listened. Then after a good visit everybody left and said good bye. They went back to their places. Gertrude and Heathcliff told everybody thank you.

After everyone left Gertrude and Heathcliff said "That was nice we have never done anything like that before. Maybe we can do it again sometime." They always talked with the turtle when he walked by since the turtle understood Heathcliff's messages. He also understood some of Gertrude's messages. When Gertrude and Heathcliff were ready to go back to Florida they always like to go there for the season, they told the turtle they were leaving and that they would be back to see him again when they came back next season. The turtle was happy and said he would look for them and that they were good friends. He would tell other turtles about them and bring them to visit next time and that he was getting ready for cold weather too. They wished he could go to Florida too but it was too far.

"Yes" said Heathcliff "We can fly and it's still very far. We always stop when we are tired and rest. Then we go again."

"Well see you next season" said the turtle.

"Ok" said Gertrude and Heathcliff "goodbye"

"Be careful" said the turtle.

"You too, be careful." And they were off flying. Heathcliff told Gertrude "We must stop by the place we always vist for a few days each time we are near there. Where the man and woman are so nice to us and always give us food to eat. You know the place with the deer and the houses."

"Oh yes."said Gertrude "We always stop there when we are near that place I like it there. Let's stop and stay there a few days.."

"Of course" said Heathcliff "We always do when we are near there. The people are always nice to us. I really like the food they give us. Remember we can even peck on their porch floor and the door for food and they feed us. They are very nice to us. We will soo n be there Gertrude."

"Oh yes there is the place. Let's stay for a few days." Said Heathcliff.

"Yes we can the weather is still nice but it is getting cool in the evening. We can still stay a few days and come back next season."

After staying at the nice place in Wisconsin for a few days Gertrude and Heathcliff left for Florida and stayed for the winder then returned in the spring. They visited their friend the turtle when they returned other friends also. Then visited the nice folks in Wisconsin brought along two fuzzy little ones also. Everyone was happy. Then one day Heathcliff did not return with Gertrude. Gertrude waited and waited. He seemed very much alone. But prepares the new owns daily for the trip to a more warm area when the season is cold. The cranes are beautiful almost magical to see.

About The Author

I'm Al Vicent, originally from Michigan.
I settled in Salinas California after military service
and enjoy writing poetry to fill the vacancy of the
seconds, minutes, and hours that occur during the
days, weeks, months, years.

Printed in the United States
By Bookmasters